✦

DANCING
WITH A GHOST

✦

DANCING WITH A GHOST

EXPLORING INDIAN REALITY

RUPERT ROSS

OCTOPUS
PUBLISHING
GROUP

Canadian Cataloguing in Publication Data

Ross, Rupert, 1946–

    Dancing with a ghost: exploring Indian reality

Includes index.

ISBN 0–409–90648–4

1. Indians of North America – Canada – Criminal justice system.   2. Indians of North America – Canada.   3. Criminal justice, Administration of – Canada.   I. Title.

KE7722.C75R6 1992   345.71′05′08997   C92–093060–3
KF8210.C7R6 1992

Sponsoring editor: Edward O'Connor

Composition, cover and text design: Joseph Chin

Copyeditor: Sheldon Fischer

Back cover photograph: Randy Kasprick

Cover painting: Cameo Shield by Hènry Letendre. Reproduced with the kind permission of the artist.

Distributed by Butterworths, 75 Clegg Road, Markham, Ontario L6G 1A1.

Published by Octopus Publishing Group, 75 Clegg Road, Markham, Ontario L6G 1A1.

Portions of this text first appeared, in a slightly different form, in the author's article "Leaving Our White Eyes Behind: The Sentencing of Native Accused." *Canadian Native Law Reporter* (1989) 3, pp. 1-15.

Printed in Canada by Webcom Limited.

TABLE OF CONTENTS

PART TWO: UNDERSTANDING THE PRESENT

FOREWORD

For years the missionaries had been pressing the Six Nations peoples and other North American Indians to forsake their manitous and uncivilized ways, and to espouse the Bible and civilization. Finally, in 1805, the Six Nations peoples granted a missionary an interview. At the end of their colloquy, Red Jacket, a celebrated Seneca orator, on behalf of the people rejected the missionaries' overture with the words in his language that meant "Kitchi-Manitou has given us a different understanding."

Although he formally represented only the Six Nations, Red Jacket's remarks applied with equal force to other North American cultures. To the people of the Six Nations and their neighbours it was quite clear even then that the notions, ideas, values, perceptions, ideals, beliefs, institutions, insights, opinions, aspirations, concepts, customs, habits, practices, conventions, outlooks—the entire tradition and way of life—that they embraced were different from those held by the newcomers.

In rejecting the invitation to conversion and preferring to abide by traditional understandings, Red Jacket did not imply that his people's understandings were better than those of the newcomers. Rather, the missionaries had not shown their beliefs and

♦

conduct to be superior to the knowledge and learning that Kitchi-Manitou had bestowed upon the Natives. And by crediting Kitchi-Manitou as the Benefactor of these understandings, Red Jacket was saying in just another way that his people's understandings possessed the same weight as those of others.

When Red Jacket uttered that one sentence, "Kitchi-Manitou has given us a different understanding," he was referring to all the differences, great and small, palpable and impalpable, that separated the Brown People and the White. Red Jacket used the pronoun "us" to convey the notion that his people collectively espoused these understandings; yet they coincided as well with each individual's own thoughts and ideas. For, even though men and women shared common beliefs and heritage, that tradition also enabled any individual to declare, "Kitchi-Manitou has given me a different understanding."

The dual public and private nature of the understandings originating with Kitchi-Manitou gave them a sacrosanct aspect. The mode by which men and women gained these understandings, through dream and vision, was also almost sacrosanct. Having their origin with Kitchi-Manitou—the Great Mystery—and coming to individuals through the mediation of the manitous, these understandings merited respect and deference.

The differences in personal perceptions and understandings were meant, it was supposed, to illuminate and enhance individual as well as general knowledge. Men and women were expected to weigh, not reject outright, opinions different from their own, and to clarify their own ideas and enrich their general understandings. It was expected that men and women, in so doing, would find merit in the ideas of others and accord those others due credit for the worth of their ideas.

Thus, although Natives were not inherently averse to examining contrary opinions, it is still true that to abandon one's opinion or belief has seldom been easy, even in the face of opinions that are clearly superior to one's own. It is doubly difficult, then, for men and women who still speak their ancestral languages to disown their cultural heritage when they can see that it is as substantive as the competing one, and still has meaning, application and purpose.

✦

And what bearing does the adherence to traditional views and customs by North American Indians have upon their relationships with this country's governments, agencies and institutions? How does the adherence to tradition bear upon the provision of government services and programs? How does adherence to traditional values bear upon national and provincial dreams and plans? How does adherence to the "old way" affect North American Indians' entry into and participation in this country's business and academic affairs?

Of course, these questions must be faced not only by Natives but by Canadians of European ancestry. How does the general unwillingness of white society to acknowledge that North American Indians have different values and institutions that have not lost their relevance and application despite five hundred years of cultural and technological advances, bear upon their affairs with the First Nations' peoples?

The answer is clear: as long as the governments and the agencies of this country fail to recognize that many original peoples of this country still cling to their different values and institutions, and so long as they insist that the original peoples abandon their ancestral heritage and embrace European culture, so long will penalties be unconsciously imposed upon the Natives and injustices and injuries be committed. And so long as the government and the officials of this country continue to act as if the original peoples are the only ones in need of instruction and improvement, so long will suspicion and distrust persist.

But if modern Canadians of European heritage were willing to grant, as their ancestors should have done two and three hundred years ago, that North American Indian values and institutions are substantive, and have the potential to add to the well-being of this country, then not only would Canadians of European ancestry benefit but everyone would gain.

Now, there are many differences between the original peoples and Canadians of overseas origin on matters of attitude, religion, customs, institutions, values, and ideals; nay, in almost every aspect of life they are poles apart. Within the limits of this Foreword only a brief sketch is possible. I will dwell briefly on three or perhaps four differences in our ways of thinking that lead

✦

to particularly adverse effects when the Euro-centric notions of justice are applied to my fellow Natives in this country. In order to ground those different views of human dignity, I must make somewhat of a discursus into the Native world view.

From the moment that European missionaries set eyes on North American Indians they assumed that the brown-skinned natives were pagan and quite incapable of grasping or expressing abstract ideas such as "God", or postulating divine attributes. The missionaries believed that at best the aboriginal mind could posit the existence of little spirits and conduct superstitious rituals and ceremonies. What the North American Indians needed was the Bible and education to draw them from the path of error and set them on the path of truth.

But the aborigines already had a word, "manitou", in the vocabulary to express the different forms of incorporeal existence. They used "manitouwun" to refer to the healing properties of a plant; "manitouwut" to refer to the mystical attributes of a natural setting; "w'manitouwih" to refer to the prophetic gift of seers. Kitchi-Manitou was God, the Great and Foremost Mystery of the supernatural and natural orders. With these terms the aborigines gave evidence of their sense that there was something more to being than physical, concrete reality.

Because Kitchi-Manitou was a being existing in the supernatural sphere, this spirit was super-ordinate to human experience, knowledge and description. But it was taken for granted and accepted as true that Kitchi-Manitou created the universe, the world and the beings upon, above, and below, both corporeal and incorporeal, from a vision or dream. Creation, by which the mystical vision was brought into the realm of physical reality, was seen as an act of generosity and a sharing of the manitou's goods with those in need.

The men and women who were created as the last and most dependent of all beings took a name in its collective form, "Anishinaubaeg", for themselves. Such a designation represented their understanding of the fundamental goodness of human nature derived from the supposition that men and women generally meant well in all their undertakings and aspirations. The name also represented the good opinion they had of themselves as men and women of merit. This belief in the essential goodness of intent of human beings remained steadfast, despite experience and the evidence of history that showed that men and women seemed more often than not to have failed to fulfill their good intentions, and did considerable harm in the process. The belief in the innate goodness of human nature remained, and conferred on men and women a sense of worth, equality, and pride.

There was another source for this sense of worth and purpose. In each person's inmost being there was implanted by Kitchi-Manitou a seed or a small clutch of talent. This was the substance that each person was to seek through dream and vision, and having taken possession of it, enhance his being, his world and his sphere with it in emulation of Kitchi-Manitou.

But to quest for a vision and then having received it, to bring it to fulfillment, has never been an easy undertaking. Human frailties such as fear and sloth, selfishness and impulsiveness, jealousy, inconstancy, conceit, irreverence, lust, and temper may dupe and withhold men and women in their quest, in their efforts to fulfill their visions. Such men and women as were discouraged or misled in their quest, or prevented from carrying out their visions or from discharging their duties and had, as a consequence, caused pain and injury, were regarded as having stumbled or lost their way or been led astray by malevolent manitous. What those who stumbled or lost their way needed was to be given a helping hand; to be redirected and counselled. Besides guidance, those who had done serious harm were expected to purify themselves in a sweat lodge and to petition the manitous for good dreams.

Apart from their presumed universal worth, Natives' practical lives had as much to do with men's and women's self-esteem. In days gone by men and women hunted, trapped, fished, harvested and prepared medicines to feed, clothe, shelter and keep themselves in good health. There was then ample opportunity for everyone to render some good service to family and community. The training, the equipment, the experience, the opportunities and the needs were similar. In such circumstances no man or woman was inferior to any other. And if further proof was needed to show or to establish the essential equality of men and women, isolation was pointed out as the one sphere in which men and women could show that they were as good, no worse than any other. To face and surmount similar challenges and tests alone, without aid, was the measure by which men and women judged others and loved to be judged. It was from service to family and community that men and women derived their sense of worth and pride. Every person was worth something, not only to himself, but to the entire community.

To set aside enough food to last them through the winter was what drove men and women to labour the summer through till the first fall of snow. If they failed to store enough food, they and their families faced hardship and the prospect of eating bark, frozen berries and moss. But if their labours had been rewarded, they could all look forward to the forthcoming winter with confidence and security. Then they could listen to tribal historians recount former accomplishments; they could listen to tribal raconteurs describe and explain the origin and nature of things and the meanings of customs, rituals, and ceremonies; and they could listen to accounts of Nanabush, the central figure in Anishinaubae literature, representing what they understood of human nature.

The Anishinaubaeg had a high regard akin to reverence for story-tellers, orators, and for language itself. The highest compliment or tribute they could pay a speaker was to say of him or her, "w'daeb-wae", taken to mean "he/she is right, correct, accurate, truthful." It is an expression approximating the word for "truth" in the English language except that it means that one casts one's knowledge as far as one has perceived it and as accurately as one can describe it, given one's command of language. In other words, the best one can do is to tell what one knows with the highest degree of accuracy. Beyond this one cannot go. According to this understanding there is or can be no such thing as absolute truth.

For the Anishinaubae peoples to predicate "w'daeb-wae" of another person was complimentary, but in so doing they were affirming that person's credibility at the same time. They were closely associating speech and credibility. It was a delicate relationship that could easily be broken by the careless use of speech. Once the bond was broken, trust and confidence in the speaker was lost. The speaker no longer had influence with an audience.

◆

For a community to regard a person as one worth listening to was the highest distinction they could confer. By the same token, the worse epithet that the Anishinaubae peoples could impose on any would-be speaker was to say "w'geewi-animoh", meaning that he or she talks in circles, as a dog barks in all directions in uncertainty as to the source of some unknown disturbance.

With this background on Native valuations of personhood and integrity, it becomes possible to understand how the whites' system of justice corrodes our view of human beings. For it is beyond doubt that among all the cultural conflicts, as sociologists call them, that have occurred wherever men and women of North American heritage meet Canadians of West European origin, none is more dramatic, or as traumatic, or as enduring as those that take place within the jurisdiction of the law and within the courts of justice.

If a man or woman has the misfortune of breaking one of the country's laws, he or she may, depending upon the gravity of the charge, be clapped into jail soon after arrest. On a lesser charge an accused may be allowed his freedom on bail. For serious offences the accused, from the moment of charge and arrest, is regarded as a felon, a criminal, a being of little worth and quite unfit to be free in the society of law-abiding citizens. That person belongs in jail—a separate "society"—with other men and women of his ilk, with the guilty and the wicked, in exile, ostracized.

But it is in the *courtroom* that the accused is systematically made to appear as a base person. The Crown introduces evidence to support its charges and to obtain a verdict of guilty, and demands the imposition of the maximum penalty, removal from the society of good men and women and sentence to the company of bad men and bad women. Counsel assails the accused's self-esteem, pride, sense of worth, and credibility. The accused's counsel may rebut the charges and obtain an acquittal, but if defence counsel is unsuccessful and the client is pronounced guilty as charged, the accused's wickedness is confirmed and upheld by the court and reported in the papers.

In the legal proceedings the accused, now a prisoner, is insignificant. Within the hierarchy of the court, the accused is consigned to the lowest place on the scale. Next in rank above him are his captors, the police officers. Still higher in standing, importance and in education are the lawyers; they are the contestants, the principal actors who command the attention of the spectators, as Perry Mason overshadowed everyone else in the television courtroom with his cleverness, wit, knowledge of the law, and eloquence. In their arguments they are, it seems, preoccupied with the accused's offence, which may have been his first and only offence, a preoccupation that magnifies the offence while burying the basic decency and good of the person in the dock. At the top and presiding over all else is the judge.

The accused, in contrast, is of little consequence; he or she is commanded to rise and to sit down, to speak and to be silent, at the behest of others. To be confined in a stall, perhaps even manacled and commanded as a slave is ordered about, is as demeaning a situation as a human being can be made to endure. It compares to what victorious warriors once did to captives—to bind them and if possible force them to perform menial labours as beasts of burden, "wukaunuk", and cast them scraps to eat. Rather than yield, many men and women defied their captors and chose torture and death.

And just as the accused is forced to put his self-esteem and dignity on the line, so must he risk his credibility. He is made to swear to "tell the truth, the whole truth, and nothing but the truth, so help you God!" And so he does, to the best of his recollection, his perceptions, and as well as his command of language enables him—and to as great or limited a degree as the lawyers want it introduced into the trial, depending on how it will advance their respective causes. But the answers the accused gives and the evidence witnesses provide are not good enough for the Crown or the accused's counsel. The lawyers are not satisfied with discrediting testimony; it seems they are intent upon destroying whoever is summoned to the dock. That they should destroy liars and perjurers is fitting. But for lawyers with the ability to make almost anyone appear like a liar and a fool to set about regularly to assault and destroy credibility is a terrible abuse of skill and authority. The accused and the witnesses are forced to run the judicial gauntlet and are made to suffer dishonour, disgrace, and even vilification at the hands of the lawyers.

What then is to be done? How avoid the ordeal? How is one to survive the ordeal in court and emerge with at least a measure of self-esteem and credibility salvaged? If the accused is innocent, will he end up in prison as did Donald Marshall and Milton Born-With-a-Tooth, or be deported and turned over to the American authorities as was Leonard Peltier, still in prison? Plead "Guilty" to be done with it quickly and with the least amount of pain seems to be the prevailing attitude.

Then suppose the accused is convicted. What hope is there for him in prison? Cast among hardened criminals, men and women deemed incorrigible, some of whom undoubtedly are, what are his prospects? In such a milieu, incarcerated with men and women who may even regard themselves as misfits, how is a person to maintain his sense of worth and pride; how is such a one to keep from losing his self-esteem and not begin believing that he is without purpose or value to himself, to his family and to his community; how is such a man or woman, cut off from kin and friends, to receive inspiration and encouragement and declaration of faith in his fundamental decency and good will? And segregated from all acquaintances, how is a prisoner to be set back on his feet if he has stumbled, or be re-directed to his way if he has gone astray?

Since the mid-sixties, many lawyers and judges have taken up the cause for the First Nations peoples, appealing for justice in the courts, and for liberality and good will in the social and economic spheres. Together the First Nations peoples and their advocates have blazed a trail some distance. There is still a long distance to go before justice is attained for all.

In *Dancing with a Ghost*, Mr. Rupert Ross has succeeded where most others have fallen short. He has succeeded in descrying some traits and habits, beliefs and insights of the Ojibway people that have eluded most scholars who are still preoccupied with social organization, hunting and fishing, food preparation, clothing, dwellings and transportation. If through this book he can convince his learned friends to look anew at the adversarial character of litigation and to examine the First Nations peoples' concept of human nature and human misconduct, and their manner of setting right an errant man or woman, he will have performed a service of great benefit in recognizing and affirming the substantiveness of these other understandings. And if by some

✦

chance, at some point beyond the present vision, the justice system of this country were to espouse and adopt the First Nations peoples' concepts and subjoin them to their own, then the administration of justice would gain a far greater measure of equity and fairness than it previously had.

Basil H. Johnston,
ORDER OF ONTARIO

PREFACE AND ACKNOWLEDGEMENTS

For many years, Native people have been asking us to acknowledge the immense gulf between our two cultures. This book is my attempt to explain, in terms which non-Natives can grasp, what I understand them to mean.

I began to write simply to articulate my confusion at the actions, reactions and explanations of Native victims and witnesses in the court process. They did not do or say the things I expected, and that perplexed me. Wanting to warn other professionals about the extent of our common ignorance, I wrote some short papers. Native people from various parts of Canada began to call, offering encouragement and explanations. It often took months of reflection to understand those explanations, so great is the gap between us.

With the encouragement of Judges Judythe Little and Donald Fraser of the Ontario Court of Justice (Provincial Division), our courts began to involve Elders, Chiefs and councillors in the sentencing of individual offenders in remote Native communities. As they spoke about their preferred responses to anti-social behaviour, their cultural homeland began to take on greater definition. Patterns began to emerge, schemes of propriety which

◆

gave new meaning to common complaints about our system of justice and our view of human relationships in general.

As I continued writing, more Native people called to assist and encourage. This book is what grew out of that process of observing, theorizing and waiting for guidance. It is offered in the hope that it will contribute to the eventual construction of bridges across the gap which separates us in so many critical ways.

Three people deserve special recognition for their contributions. The first is Dr. Clare Brant, a psychiatrist and a Mohawk from the Tyendinaga Reserve in southern Ontario. With feet in both worlds and an abiding concern for (and pride in) his people, he has dedicated a major portion of his time to increasing communication and understanding between Native and non-Native people. In particular, his articulation of traditional ethics opened a great many analytical doors for me. I will never forget reading some his work for the first time, for it had the effect of suddenly making comprehensible a vast number of incidents which had always puzzled me. Without those keys, I would still be stumbling around in cross-cultural darkness, unable to see any of the behavioural patterns which give the traditional Native worldview its unique structure. I hope I have done his work justice. Thank you, Clare, on behalf of all people trying to learn.

If Clare Brant opened the doors for me, the man who helped me walk through them was Charlie Fisher, an Elder from the Islington Reserve at Whitedog Falls in northwestern Ontario, and Ontario's first full-time Native Justice of the Peace. For four years Charlie and I hopped aboard small aircraft and ventured into the remote Native communities of the region, conducting courts dealing with breaches of band bylaws, particularly those dealing with the ravages of alcohol abuse. I listened as he spoke with people, as he tried to bring healing to them, as he looked behind their substance abuse to examine the underlying causes. I watched as he struggled to make our law productive in those communities.

Just as importantly, I felt Charlie watching me and, in his gentle way, educating me to traditionally proper behaviour. Loyal to his cultural commandments, Charlie never criticized what I did nor told me directly how to conduct myself. Instead, he told me stories as we flew from place to place. In time I learned how

◆

to listen to those stories, how to see beyond their casual appearance. To say that they contained lessons would be wrong; instead, they crystallized various scenarios within which some choices would clearly be wise and others inappropriate. The ultimate choice, however, would always be mine. From Charlie, then, I learned how to listen, for he never gave up hope that my blunt westerner's mind might slow down and be alert to nuance.

From learning how to listen, I slowly learned how to speak (and to be silent!) so that I might be better able to join in real communication with the people of the North. Over time, Charlie carefully put me into more and more complex situations both in court and out of it, requiring me to "earn my learning" in the traditional way. At all times, however, I felt him there, somewhere beside me, ready to help out if my blunders threatened to cause too much damage, but also ready to let me learn by my own mistakes. In this way I regularly felt his love, not just for me, but for all learners (which, in Native terms, means all people). He once said he considered the two of us, when we went into the North, to be a team; it may be the greatest compliment I will ever receive. Megwetch, Charlie.

Thirdly, I must also express my appreciation to E.C. "Ted" Burton, the Regional Director of Crown Attorneys for northwestern Ontario, who retired in the summer of 1991. He had the faith to hire me as a Crown Attorney and send me into the North just as courts were expanding into remote Native communities. He encouraged me to experiment with community involvement in the court system. Most importantly, he conveyed to me his own certainty, drawn from many years in the North, that there was much to prize in traditional Native teachings. Though his job as Regional Director required that he move from Kenora to Thunder Bay, he was a regular voice on the telephone, swapping stories, speculation and theory, joining with me in the exploration I've tried to write about here.

Just as importantly, Ted was able to persuade our Ministry to support my travel to Native justice conferences where even more learning took place, and he backed my efforts to put my experiences and theories on paper. We've never travelled the North together, but I've always felt him at my side. Thanks, Ted.

✦

Many other people were of invaluable assistance in a variety of ways, including: Richard Cummine (Crown Attorney, Kenora); Josias Fiddler (Coordinator, Sandy Lake Justice Project); Judges Judythe Little and Donald Fraser (Ontario Court, Provincial Division, Kenora); Don Hewitt (Ontario Provincial Police, Northwest Patrol Unit, Sioux Lookout, Ontario); Stan Jolly (Policy Analyst, Ontario Ministry of the Attorney General); Douglas Hunt, Q.C. (former Assistant Deputy Attorney General, Ontario); T. Ambrose O'Flaherty, Q.C. (lawyer, Kenora); Abel Rae (Elder, Sandy Lake, Ontario); Bruce Sealy (retired educator, Winnipeg); Mary Schantz (former staff, Ontario Native Affairs Directorate); Albert Tootoosis (Native Courtworker, Edmonton); Sylvia Novik (Special Advisor, Alberta Solicitor General); Cathy Louis (National Parole Board); Chester Cunningham (Director, Native Counselling Services of Alberta); Judge James Igliolorte (Provincial Court, Labrador); Walter Linklater (Thunder Bay); Joe Cardinal (Cree Elder, Alberta); Maggie Strachan (whose Master's Thesis on Native people and right brain/left brain capabilities jump-started recollections of pattern-thought from my guiding days); and the unidentified wordsmith who coined a phrase that has, on rare occasions, given comfort: "When you try to be a bridge between two cultures, you should expect to get walked over by some people from both sides."

And Val, who shares my fascination and constantly supports my work.

Thank you, all.

Rupert Ross
Kenora, Ontario

✦

*I*NTRODUCTION

In 1968 I left Toronto to take a summer job as a fishing guide in northwestern Ontario, north of Kenora. There were only about three hundred people in the village that was to become my home for the next nineteen years. Half of them were Native, and their condition was a shock to me. In the summer they lived in tents along the river; in the winter their shelter came from shacks or crude log cabins. Their daily lives were characterized by a degree of poverty, violence and alcohol abuse I had never encountered before.

Questions arose in my mind. Who are these people? Why do they live this way? Can nothing be done?

Those questions have stayed with me ever since. I continued guiding for the next eleven years, but in 1977 I enrolled in law school. In 1982 I began to practice in Kenora, quickly choosing to specialize in criminal law. Over eighty percent of my clients were Native, and as I worked with them my curiosity grew. Then, just as court services were being expanded into the remote, fly-in reserves of the region, a job came open as Assistant Crown Attorney. I applied for and got that job, volunteering to take on those new courts. As a result, I have been hopping into small aircraft and heading north some three days out of every week since 1985. While

◆

a good portion of my time in those communities is spent in court, my duties also involve working with Elders, Chiefs and councillors to try to improve both the court system and the internal responses of the communities to anti-social activities.

The same questions, however, remain. More to the point, they still remain largely unanswered. The more that I listen, watch and learn, the less I feel certain I really understand.

I am now drawn to the conclusion that while we share with Native people a common desire to live healthy, love-filled and peaceful lives, we share very few concepts about *how* to accomplish those goals. Our two cultures are, in my view, separated by an immense gulf, one which the Euro-Canadian culture has never recognized, much less tried to explore and accommodate.

Not a day goes by that I don't catch new glimpses of how foreign and elusive Native rules of behaviour are to me. In turn, each new glimpse promises that there will be still further surprises. On a daily basis I am faced with an expanding awareness of my own ignorance.

In retrospect, the discovery of such a gulf should not have been surprising. The fact that it was suggests that I must have carried an assumption with me into the North, the assumption that Indians were probably just "primitive versions" of us, a people who needed only to "catch up" to escape the poverty and despair which afflicts far too many of their communities.

That assumption is both false and dangerous. We would never carry it into China or Tibet or any other obviously foreign place. Instead, we would approach the people of those lands with an expectation of profound difference and a sincere determination to learn and accommodate. To date, that has not been the predominant approach of Canadians to Native people on this continent.

They are not just different versions of us. They began their journey to today not where we did, with the Mediterranean world-view classically enunciated by Plato and Aristotle. They began it in Asia, then brought that Asian world-view to the reality of a harsh, nomadic existence on this land mass many thousands of years before Plato was born. They developed, refined and sustained it over those centuries, *and it sustained them.* The paths they followed were completely different from ours as we

✦

passed through the rise and fall of Greece and Rome, the
Christian Middle Ages, the Renaissance, the development of a
wage and money economy, secularization, and the growth of
major cities. For most Indians of the North, even the Industrial
Revolution took place without their knowledge or direct involvement. If we recall that, apart from the occasional missionary and
trapper, the Native people of northwestern Ontario had no sustained, significant contact with the "outside" until some twenty
or thirty years ago, we should not be surprised that we have difficulties communicating with each other. The wonder is that there
has been any successful communication at all.

What follows is a personal, decidedly non-academic attempt to
deal with our communication failure and with those questions
which first arose, for me, in 1968. To some extent, it consists of
no more than unsophisticated guesswork on my part, for I suspect
that it is virtually impossible to climb inside the world-view of
another culture. This may be especially true when it is a city -
raised white man of the post-industrial world (and a lawyer to
boot) who is trying to do it. The points of divergence are virtually
everywhere.

   I therefore apologize at the outset to Native people, for I am
very likely to misrepresent you. I cannot help but see you through
my own culture's eyes. I have had the benefit of many kind and
patient teachers from among you, and they have done their best,
in their gentle and elliptical way, to lead me into clear vision, but
my eyes are not yours. I am at least aware that I am largely
unaware of your shadings and subtleties, of the real sophistica-
tion of your social structures. I will no doubt draw conclusions
which you will find laughingly — or insultingly — incorrect. *I am
convinced, however, that we have no choice but to start talking
about such things.*

   I offer what follows not in the hope that it will suddenly
explain Native people to others. It can't, and it won't. Instead, it
is offered to help make the majority culture aware of how chroni-
cally ignorant we are of the very complex world Native people
inhabit. My wish is to underline, at least, the fact that we have
not approached Native people with the expectation of difference

✦

which is essential for communication and understanding to commence. Not having perceived that a gulf divides us, we have never truly tried to bridge it. Unless we do, it is my fear that we are doomed to increasing mutual frustration and, as we have already seen with the armed confrontation between Native people and our police and military at Oka, Quebec, in the summer of 1990, overt hostilities.

If, as I hope, my guesswork helps to bring some definition to the gulf which both separates and threatens us, I will be more than pleased.

I strongly caution the reader to approach what follows with two caveats in mind. First, my experience has been primarily with the Cree and Ojibway peoples of northwestern Ontario. Hunter-gatherer traditions are still strong. What application that experience has to agricultural or coastal Native people I am not able to say. Reaction to a shorter, early draft of the book by Native people from Labrador to the Yukon, however, suggested a marked similarity in fundamental approaches from coast to coast.

Second, each of the communities familiar to me is unique. None has remained untouched by the outside world, but each has been touched in different ways and for different periods of time. Similarly, individuals within each community have had very different kinds and degrees of contact with the outside. On any one reserve you can find some who have been out to university and some who, in the words of one band councillor, are "stone-age people, pre-agrarian, pre-industrial, who think only in the Old Ways". It is therefore absurd to pretend to describe "Indians", for each person will occupy a unique position on the continuum of adaptation from the Old Ways to new ways which are still in the making. The same holds true for entire communities as they struggle to find a new social consensus; their evolving approaches are much more varied than many outsiders might suspect.

The generalizations that follow, then, are no more than that. They are unlikely to describe with accuracy any one Native person or any one Native community. Every Native person in Canada will be entitled to feel misrepresented in one way or another by what I have written.

That being said, however, it remains critical, in my view, that

✦

we begin the process of trying to explain ourselves to each other in terms that the other can understand. For my own part, it is much better that, for the purpose of trying to achieve real understanding, we be loudly inaccurate than silent, that we expose ourselves to the risk of being soundly rebuffed rather than perpetuate undisturbed ignorance. We cannot continue acting as we have. Since contact was first established, the majority culture has taken "assistance" measures which, in many instances, were profoundly counter-productive because we either failed to perceive the issues accurately, or because our remedies required Native people to take steps which only we would take, within our own definitions of propriety. Those steps were most frequently not proper for Native people, with the result that they were not taken at all or, in being attempted, only compounded the problem.

Many of the differences to be sketched here cast doubt on the capacity of our institutions to deal effectively with Native realities, and so appear to be arguments in favour of self-government. Others will challenge (as many Native communities are themselves challenging) the wisdom of retaining some formerly central elements of traditional culture, and so appear to be arguments in favour of assimilation. It is not my purpose to promote either position. I suspect, in fact, that it is not an either-or dynamic, that there exists a third possibility: the building, over time, of a Canadian culture which includes elements of both cultures.

I also hope to underline the degree to which many Native people find the rest of us foreign and perplexing. Never realizing that a gulf divides us, we have never stopped to explain ourselves to them. Instead, we blithely make pronouncements about what we will do for them and then impose our structures and institutions without ever explaining why we built them and how we believe they will produce the desired results. There is mutual bewilderment here, based on a mutual assumption only now being proved wrong: the assumption that both societies shared common notions of the "proper" way to relate to and treat the universe, other people, and one's own mental and spiritual health.

What has not, to date, been mutual, is accommodation between the two cultures. That has been a one-way street, with all the concessions coming from Native people.

✦

It is time things changed. It is time the gulf between us was acknowledged, explored, bridged where possible and accommodated where not. Neither group is going to disappear. We must both deal with our unresolved feelings of grief, anger and guilt before we can recognize that the future is our *common* challenge. It is essential that we start explaining ourselves to each other so that we can make choices for the future—together and separately—based on accurate perceptions of the two realities. Perhaps then we can begin to leave the pattern of the past behind.

Finally, I should provide a warning about the structure of the exploration that follows. I found it extremely difficult to locate either a beginning or an end to the description. The narrative will appear to wander from one issue to another, then back again. It will touch on some themes many times. Each re-visiting will, I hope, provide a refinement, expansion or critical modification of what was said before. It is not the way in which we are accustomed to examining things, and I ask for your patience. It is the inter-connectedness of every part which makes a complete description of any one part in isolation an impossible task.

As I wrote, I kept seeing a certain image. It was as though "Indian Reality" was itself a very large, circular room sitting in complete darkness. That room had hundreds of doors. Opening one door let some light in, but not enough to penetrate more than a few feet without being swallowed up. Opening a second door not only shed light on *its* pathway but spilled some over to the first as well. Each time I returned to that room and opened another door, I was better able to see what lay inside. And so the process continued. As I learned new things, more light fell on things I'd only partially, or even mistakenly, glimpsed before.

So progress in this exploration was a circular affair, with advances on one front permitting advances on all fronts if the time was taken to re-visit them. In the end, with as many doors open as possible, a sense of the whole began to emerge. Not only was that whole greater than the sum of its parts; none of the parts could be fully understood without reference to the whole.

It is for these reasons that I was unable to construct the narrative in a straightforward, linear fashion. Early chapters correspond to first doors being opened. They contain first glimpses, or first guesses, and they are potentially misleading when taken alone. As the chapters progress, greater light will be shed on certain issues and themes, and their significance will change. I therefore ask for suspension of final judgement until the narrative is complete.

Chapters 5 and 6 pose special problems. They go beyond a simple exploration of the ethics and rules of traditional times, to look at how those practices came to be. They move into a discussion of a phenomenon common to many peoples around the globe who live a hunter-gatherer existence: a belief system centred upon the existence of a spiritual plane lying parallel to, and interacting with, the physical one. As such, those chapters go beyond my primary task of trying to describe what was and what remains, focussing instead upon how they first came to be. It is my conviction, however, that the full force of that belief system and its impact upon the ordering of everyday life are critical to even a partial understanding of Native reality.

Enough preamble. Let the exploration begin. I hope you enjoy following my struggles as much as I, in the end, enjoyed experiencing them.

Fly-in Native communities served by the Ontario Court of Justice (Provincial Division) out of Kenora, Ontario.

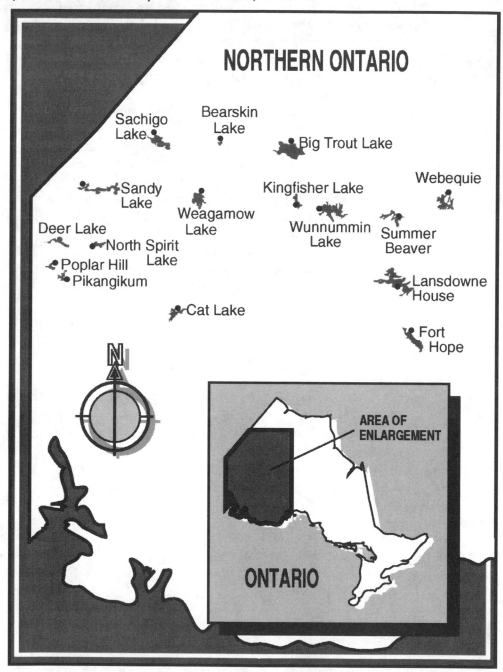

NORTHERN ONTARIO

Sachigo Lake
Bearskin Lake
Big Trout Lake
Webequie
Sandy Lake
Kingfisher Lake
Weagamow Lake
Wunnummin Lake
Summer Beaver
Deer Lake
North Spirit Lake
Poplar Hill
Pikangikum
Lansdowne House
Cat Lake
Fort Hope

N

AREA OF ENLARGEMENT

ONTARIO

PART ONE

EXCAVATING
TRADITIONAL
REALITY

■

CHAPTER 1

SEEING THROUGH THE RULES

I can think of no better way to begin than by retelling a story told to me by Dr. Clare Brant, a Mohawk from Tyendinaga in southern Ontario, who has been one of my two most helpful Native mentors over the last several years.

In the 1970s, he said, his Mohawk band hosted a sporting tournament to which they invited a group of James Bay Cree. The Mohawk, who were an agricultural people long before contact with Europeans, had developed a custom of always setting out considerably more food than their guests could consume. In this way they demonstrated both their wealth and their generosity. The Cree, however, had a different custom. A hunter-gatherer people for whom scarcity was a daily fact, their custom involved always eating everything that was set before them. In this way they demonstrated their respect for the successful hunter and for his generosity.

Needless to say, a problem arose when these two sets of rules came into collision. The Cree, anxious to show respect, ate and ate until they were more than a little uncomfortable. They considered the Mohawk something akin to gastro-intestinal sadists intent on poisoning them. The Mohawk, for their part, thought the Cree ill-mannered people intent on insulting Mohawk generosity.

✦

What is of interest in this story is not simply the collision of social customs. That might well be expected. The significant point is that each group believed that the other was *intentionally* being insulting and disrespectful when, in fact, each group had been going to great pains (especially the Cree!) to show exactly the opposite. The problem lay in the fact that each group could only see the other through its own rules, could only interpret the behaviour of others from within their own perspective.

Acts are never merely acts. They are also signals of attitude. Those signals, however, are often culture specific. When acts are seen, but their signal-content misinterpreted, it is impossible to avoid forming inaccurate interpretations of others. Until we understand what particular acts *mean* to the other, we will continually ascribe motivations and states of mind which are well off the mark. As in the Cree-Mohawk débâcle, the two groups will go away believing that the other was deliberately trying to insult them.

As a second illustration, I want to pass on something taught me by my other significant Native mentor, Charlie Fisher, an Elder from the Islington Reserve at Whitedog Falls in northwestern Ontario, and Ontario's first full-time, salaried Native Justice of the Peace. Several years ago Charlie and I had just finished a court session on a remote reserve, one in which a community Elder had again been of invaluable assistance by advising the court on appropriate sentences for each offender. I had gone up to him, looked him straight in the eye, shook his hand and told him, in effusive terms, how much I appreciated his contribution. I learned from Charlie that I had made two basic errors.

First, he advised, verbal expressions of praise and gratitude are embarrassing and impolite, especially in the presence of others. The proper course is to quietly ask the person to *continue* making his contribution next time around.

Second, looking someone straight in the eye, at least among older people in that community, was a rude thing to do. It sends a signal that you consider that person in some fashion inferior. The proper way to send a signal of respect was to look down or to the side, with only occasional glances up to indicate attention. I had been trying to say one thing but had done so in a way which conveyed exactly the opposite. To my great relief, Charlie also assured me that the man had probably not taken offence; he knew, after all, that a great many white men simply hadn't learned how to behave in a civilized fashion!

When Charlie told me that sustaining direct eye contact was frequently considered rude, I was swamped with memories of countless Native victims and witnesses who, almost without exception, had taken the witness stand and refused to look anyone in the eye. Instead, they alternated between staring off into the distance and giving us only the most fleeting of glances. In doing so, they had meant to send messages of attention and respect. The messages received by the non-Native court personnel, however, were exactly the opposite ones. Within our culture (and especially the culture of the courtroom) we are trained to see such behaviour as evasive. We discount what people say when they won't hold our eyes, concluding most often that they are insincere and untrustworthy as witnesses. I wondered how many true stories we had dismissed simply because we saw those people through the lens of our own culture, never once suspecting that the act of turning away the eyes might mean something entirely different in another culture.

I also found myself remembering a phrase that became popular with my own generation in the mid-sixties, one coined by the Scottish psychiatrist R.D. Laing in his book *The Politics of Experience*. As he expressed it, "Until you can see through the rules, you can only see through the rules." I interpret that proposition in this way: until you understand that your own culture dictates how you translate everything you see and hear, you will never be able to see or hear things in any *other* way. The first step in coming to terms with people of another culture, then, is to acknowledge that we constantly *interpret* the words and acts of others, and that we do so subconsciously but always in conformity with the way which our culture has taught us is the "proper" way. The second step involves trying to gain a conscious understanding of what those culture-specific rules might be. Until that happens, it is impossible for us to admit that our interpretation of the behaviour of someone from another culture might be totally erroneous.

I suspect that it is commonplace for signals to be misread when Native and non-Native people meet, commonplace for each of us to hear things which the other never intended, and to go away with entirely mistaken impressions. We are not aware that we act within conventional sets of rules ourselves. We assume instead that the way we behave, express ourselves, and interpret others is the way all people do it. All cultures operate with this myopia, it seems to me, not even suspecting that others may have developed very different rules.

What the two stories illustrate is that both groups in a meeting of cultures have an obligation to *expect* difference, to expect that our interpretations of the other's words and acts are liable to be incorrect. Above all else, whenever we find ourselves beginning to draw negative conclusions from what the other has said or done, we must take the time to step back and ask whether those words and acts might be open to different interpretations, whether that other person's actions may have a different meaning from within his cultural conventions.

This, then, is the nature of the task at hand: learning to go beyond what we think we see and hear to ask what a person from a different culture and with a different sense of reality is truly trying to tell us.

As a final introductory note I'd like to quote a sentence I copied from the blackboard at the band hall on the Weagamow Lake Reserve some 380 air miles north of Thunder Bay, Ontario: "I believe you understand what you think I said, but I'm not sure you realize that what you heard is not what I meant."

I have no idea who those words were directed to, but I'd be willing to bet they were aimed at someone, who, like me, probably didn't even understand what the warning was all about.

CHAPTER 2

SIGNALS
OF DIFFERENCE

Most of my contact with Native people has been in the courts. It was, consequently, the behaviour of Native victims, witnesses, and accused which provided me with the first substantial signals of cultural difference.

If I have one overriding impression of those people, it is of *silent* people. They rarely speak easily with me in private, and even less easily in court. I have watched them take the witness stand only to pull their jackets over their heads and stand there, shrouded and mute. Even when they have gone over their evidence with me in great detail before going into court, they regularly refuse to speak once they take the witness stand.

The question, of course, is why? Until that is answered, we have no idea what to do next. If we are wrong in our explanation, we are very likely to respond wrongly, making things worse for everyone instead of better.

When I first encountered this reaction of silence and with-drawal, I interpreted it in my own way. I thought of a number of possible explanations. Fear of reprisal by the ones they were testi-fying against might be one of them, or fear of the complex and foreign procedures of the court. I thought, as well, of the embar-

✦

6

rassment of disclosing personal events in a public forum, and of the natural pain which accompanies the reliving of traumatic events. I thought of the possibility that forgiveness had replaced blame, for it is not unheard of for victims and their assailants to come to terms with each other; I know of one instance where a rape victim later married the man convicted of raping her. Reluctance to speak out in court can also result if the initial complaint was either exaggerated or fabricated, that is, from an unwillingness to repeat a lie when put under oath. In fact, all those reasons are likely to be operative in Native witnesses, just as they are in others, and I believe that they were the operative reasons on many occasions when witnesses refused to speak.

Gradually, though, I began to see and hear things which made me suspect that there might exist a whole range of different explanations where Native people are concerned. One young victim of a rape refused to testify because, as she put it, "It's not right to do this after so much time. He should be finished with it now and getting on with his life." She was sixteen years old.

Another woman, the victim of a violent assault by her dangerous nephew, went over her evidence with me in great detail just before court. She insisted (uncharacteristically, I should add) that I do whatever I could to send this uncontrollably violent young man out of the community for as long as possible so that she and her children could live in peace. When she took the witness stand minutes later, however, her refusal to say anything at all about the attack led to his acquittal.

In another case, after a lengthy review of her evidence, the victim, a fifteen-year-old who had been sexually assaulted by her former boyfriend, told me she thought she could repeat her story in court. As we walked into the courtroom, though, she tugged at my sleeve and asked, "Should I say these things in court? Is it right?"

"Is it right?" That was a dumbfounding question for me. I knew of many significant reasons which made it difficult for people to testify, but it had never occurred to me that in their eyes it might not be the *right* thing to do. I had always assumed that even the most frightened and reluctant witness shared my conviction that testifying was what they should do, even if competing concerns made it impossible for them to go through with it.

✦

What, I asked myself, if we are wrong in that assumption when we deal with Native people? Could they actually believe that coming forward in this fashion was an improper thing to do? If that was the case, then factors such as fear or embarrassment only reinforced the basic disinclination.

It was not until 1986, at a conference in Whitehorse dealing with Native justice issues, that I began to see a little further into the dynamics of such reluctance. It was commonly agreed by the conference participants that Native people, with their belief in consensus decision-making, might find our adversarial system foreign and inappropriate. To explore alternate forms of dealing with social disruption we play-acted a more informal mediation process. In this exercise we devised a scenario in which a youth had broken into the community store and vandalized it. We selected some volunteers from the audience to act as the boy, the store manager and the mediation panel. That panel then asked them both about the break-in, the value of the damage, about how they felt towards each other, and about what could be done to set matters straight between them. It seemed a sensible alternative approach.

One of the mediators, however, was Charlie Fisher, whom I mentioned in Chapter 1. He was asked if such a technique bore any resemblance to what might have been done at Whitedog in more traditional times. His response was a very vehement "no" He then volunteered to make the appropriate changes.

He began by getting rid of the chairs and tables; everyone sat on the floor in a circle, as equals. He then asked for two other people to act as "Representing Elders", one each for the boy and the store manager. As he continued, it became clear that our little experiment in non-adversarial mediation was flawed in virtually every respect. In Charlie's version, the boy and the store manager never spoke in the presence of the panel of Elders. There was no discussion whatever about the break-in, the damage, the feelings of the disputants, or what might be done to set matters straight. There was no *talk* of compensation or restitution, much less the actual imposition of such measures.

Once we understood what was *not* going to take place, we had only one question left: "Why, then, is there a panel at all?"

✦

Charlie Fisher tried to answer us in this way. The duty of each Representing Elder, he explained, was not to speak for the young man or the store manager, but to counsel them in private. That counselling was intended to help each person "rid himself of his bad feelings". Such counselling would continue until the Elder was satisfied that "the person's spirit had been cleansed and made whole again". When the panel convened, an Elder could signify that such cleansing had taken place by touching the ceremonial pipe. The panel would continue to meet until both Elders so signified. At that point, the pipe would be lit and passed to all. As far as the community was concerned, that would be the end of the matter. Whether the two disputants later arranged recompense of some sort was entirely up to them. Passing the pipe signified, as Charlie phrased it, that each had been "restored to the community and to himself".

What was going on here? No fact finding? No allocation of responsibility? No imposition of consequences? Weren't these the very things our courts were created to do? Why didn't the Whitedog people do them in traditional times?

Another conference participant then told us about how such things were handled traditionally in her tiny Inuit village. The entire village assembled, including the two parties involved. An Elder would say, "I want us all to think about what should happen if a certain kind of problem were to arise." He would then go on to describe what had in fact happened, but it would be treated by everyone as a fictional event, as something that *might* happen in the future. Everyone, including the two disputants, would then be expected to make suggestions about how such a problem might be avoided in the first place, about how people might change their approaches to minimize such frictions. No one pointed fingers at anyone else, with the result that no one became "the accused" and no one became "the victim". In this way no one in the community had to come forward and speak of the event publicly in an accusatory fashion. The meeting was, instead, conducted as a theoretical discussion where everyone's wisdom was important.

There are several things of interest about such techniques. First, the victim never had to speak of the trauma or trouble in the presence of the person who had caused it. Second, the accused was never singled out publicly to become an accused at all; no labelling took place. Third, the tribunal, or community, never imposed consequences upon anyone.

I began to wonder whether the silence of the victims with whom I had dealt had its roots in a system of ethics and traditional processes about which I was completely ignorant. More questions arose. Why was it that victims were so carefully protected from having to say accusatory things in public? Why was that, apparently, an inappropriate thing to require of them? Obviously, they were able to speak of such things in some context, for if they hadn't, then the disputes would never have become known; no one would have known whom to call before the Whitedog Elders or what hypothetical event to put before the Inuit villagers for their consideration. Had I not also been told by numerous Elders that before the courts came to the North the central social mechanism for keeping order was gossip? And was it not true that victims in my own legal experience seemed, by and large, unafraid of reporting problems to the community police?

The critical distinguishing factor seemed to be the whereabouts of the accused. Once he or she was present, the cloak of silence descended. A central rule in our British-based court system, dating back to the trial of Sir Walter Raleigh in the seventeeth century, requires precisely the opposite. Raleigh asserted that he had the right, if accused of some transgression, to have the accuser "say it to my face". When the courts agreed with that demand, the hearsay rule came into existence. Gossip is excluded from court; no one can come to court to repeat what a witness has told him. The witness must appear in person and tell his or her story directly—in the presence of the accused. It is a central rule of our court system to this day. From my experience in the North, however, it began to appear that there was a central Native ethic which declared the contrary: "Say it to anyone you like, even go on the community radio and gossip about it, but never say it to the person's face." If this was true, where did this principle come from, and how did it operate?

✦

CHAPTER 3

THE RULES OF TRADITIONAL TIMES

The question raised by witnesses' refusal to testify suggested the possibility that our two societies might be built upon some very different principles, and these are the subject of this chapter. I confess that were it not for Dr. Clare Brant, a Mohawk, and a practicing psychiatrist who has spent a great deal of time exploring the underpinnings of both traditional and present-day Native societies, I would probably find myself still stumbling around in the dark, aware that I was on foreign terrain but without a map to guide me. As luck would have it, however, I ran across a transcript of a speech he gave to Native parents in southern Ontario some years ago, and the analytical doors began to open.* In that speech he canvassed a number of rules or ethics which he suggests were central to the conduct of Native life in traditional times and which, to varying degrees, remain important today.

---

*Clare Brant, "Living, Loving, Hating Families in the '80s." Address delivered at the Oshweken Community Hall, January 9, 1982.

◆

A. THE ETHIC OF NON-INTERFERENCE

To begin, I cannot do better than to quote directly from Dr.Brant. It is his view that the dominant ethic is one which he calls the Ethic of Non-Interference.

> The Ethic of Non-Interference is probably one of the oldest and one of the most pervasive of all the ethics by which we Native people live. It has been practised for twenty-five or thirty thousand years, but it is not very well articulated. The person who [explained] it best was a white woman, an anthropologist, named Rosalie Wax, when she published a paper in 1952 called "Indians and White People". This principle essentially means that an Indian will never interfere in any way with the rights, privileges and activities of another person.
>
> I'll have to expand on that and explain it by comparing it with white people and the way they operate. In every human relationship there is some element of influence, interference or even downright compulsion. The white man is torn between two ideals. On the one hand, he believes in freedom, in minding his own business and in the right of people to make up their minds for themselves. On the other hand, he believes he should be his brother's keeper and not abstain from giving advice or even taking action when he perceives his brother making an error.
>
> Thus, at a white person's cocktail party, when someone announces that he wishes to buy a pear tree, he can usually expect someone to suggest he buy a peach tree instead. Someone will be glad, in a friendly way of course, to tell him what he should be reading, doing, talking, feeling, listening to, etc. The Indian society does not allow this. Interference in any form is forbidden, regardless of the following irresponsibility or mistakes that your brother is going to make.
>
> This principle can be illustrated further by the example of Indian people riding in a car. If the car is the property of the driver, no Indian will ever think of giving the driver instructions, even if a deer or a rockslide blocks the right-of-way. To do so would be interfering with the activities and freedom of

another. This is forbidden, rude, and will not usually be done by the Indian person.

This principle of non-interference is all-pervasive through-out our entire culture. *We are very loath to confront people. We are very loath to give advice to anyone if the person is not specifically asking for advice. To interfere or even com-ment on their behaviour is considered rude.* (emphasis added)

After reading a transcript of Dr. Brant's speech, I began to understand that some of my questions could only be answered by placing them within a different cultural context. There is no doubt that giving evidence is confrontational; we intentionally structure it that way. It is criticism of someone's behaviour in the extreme. Perhaps the refusal of witnesses to participate in our consciously adversarial courts sprang from an adherence to ethi-cal commandments whose existence I had never glimpsed. Certainly the refusal of Elders to impose consequences could be seen in a cultural context, for doing such a thing would have been tantamount to an "institutional" breach of the ethic forbidding interference in the lives of others.

I began to feel that there might be some validity to my suspi-cion that for many Native people testifying in court might actually be a *wrong* thing to do. When they repeatedly asked me why they had tell their story over again in court when they had already told "us" (meaning me and the police), they were not just trying to avoid an unpleasant experience; they were trying to avoid participation in what they considered an immoral one. For many of them, testifying against someone to his or her face in a public courtroom may well have seemed an even greater wrong than what was done to them in the first place (especially when the accused had acted in a drunken state, while the witness, in contrast, was being asked to act with full and sober deliberation).

In passing, I would also like to note a corollary ethic. It has to do with truth-telling, with acknowledging your misdeeds and in that way seeking to restore or maintain your welcome in the group. For the Mohawk, lying has always been one of the most serious crimes, and lying for them apparently includes attempting

✦

to deny or minimize one's own behaviour. "Convictions" for lying (and the Mohawk possessed a very elaborate, impartial and institutionalized justice system long before the first Europeans arrived) followed one for life, and upon the third such finding the consequence was banishment. Among all Native groups with whom I have worked there appears to be nothing akin to our "right to silence", our right to refuse to incriminate ourselves. On the contrary, there appears to be an opposite commandment, one that requires full disclosure, full acknowledgement of wrongs. It is apparently seen as an essential first step towards rehabilitation and the reintegration into the community. It may be that this ethic contributes substantially to the high frequency of guilty pleas by Native accused. At the very least, it contributes to a high rate of full confessions during police questioning, and these confessions are often what lead defence counsel to the conclusion that a plea of "Not Guilty" would be fruitless.

I have also regularly watched Native accused show clear discomfort when they enter pleas of "Not Guilty" upon the advice of their lawyers, especially where the court is taking place in their home community. We have not been successful in explaining that such a plea does not amount to the outright denial it appears to be, but is merely a way of stating that you require the Crown to prove the charge under the law beyond a reasonable doubt. Even if that difference is fully understood, I suspect that for many Native accused putting such an onus on the community by requiring witnesses to come forward and testify would still be seen as an immoral thing to do. The rule is *not* to burden others in that way.

As strong as this general rule against criticising others to their face may be, it carries greater force still when family members are involved. Dr. Brant suggests that it is wrong even to think critical or angry thoughts in those circumstances. In the same speech from which I quoted earlier, he put it this way.

> I saw at one outpost in the Moose Factory zone [on James Bay] an Indian fellow who, the night before, had beaten his wife to the point that she had to be hospitalized with fractures and internal bleeding. He then took an axe and demolished the inside of his house. I went to examine him,

✦

as a psychiatrist. I was interested in knowing why he was so angry with his wife. He said "I wasn't angry, I was drunk." I said, "She must have provoked you in some way. She must have given rise to an enormous rage inside you to provoke you to nearly kill her and then destroy the property that you have slaved and laboured over the past fifteen years to construct." But he was unwilling to see, unwilling to say that he was angry with his wife. ... He never did actually admit that this woman did have aggravating habits which he felt needed to be changed.

It is Dr. Brant's view that the ethic prohibiting criticism is often so strongly held that it cannot be breached even when such a confession is encouraged by a professional helper.

This approach to human relations seems wholly foreign to the one I see in my own culture. We have built institutions to reflect our different cultural imperatives. For one, we have built courts dedicated to adversarial fact finding, the public allocation of blame, and the imposition of consequences, including punishment. We have also built psychiatric hospitals premised on our belief that it is both right and productive to explore, express, define and direct our deepest feelings, especially those of a hostile nature. We strongly encourage people to meet face-to-face, to be open and direct about what aggravates them. Assuming that our approaches are universally applicable, we offer such institutions to Native people. When they don't work, we assume it is because Natives don't want them to work. They, by the same token, initially accept these institutions in the belief that they represent versions of their own. When that proves not to be the case, when they realize that continued participation in them requires that they break their own ethical codes at virtually every step along the way, they respond with passive but determined resistance. The more that we insist that they use our approaches and institutions, the more they conclude that we are trying to intentionally destroy their rules and ethics, their culture, by imposing our own. Both groups slide into resentful puzzlement at the apparent intransigence of the other.

✦

The Ethic of Non-Interference is most dramatically evident in the context of child-rearing, and it is precisely here that a white person finds it most difficult to believe that there is any ethic working at all. In essence, traditional rules required parents to permit their children to make their own choices in virtually every aspect of life. In the contemporary world, it stands as a requirement that parents let their children decide what is best in everything, from bedtimes, clothing, and school attendance to selection of friends, and eating habits. Nor can parents "teach" their children in our sense of the word, by either words or special demonstration. Instead, children must learn on their own, by watching and by emulating what they see. Dr. Brant terms this the "modelling" approach to education, an approach to be used whether the task is as simple as putting on a pair of trousers or as complex as mending a canoe. There can be no cajolery, no praise or punishment, no withholding of privileges or promising of rewards. It is up to the child to observe constantly and carefully, to study entirely on their own. In Dr. Brant's own case, at the age of fourteen and with no prior instruction except for sitting at his father's side atop their farm tractor, he was simply told that it was his turn to drive. His father expected him to have learned merely by watching, and to be ready to perform with excellence.

Dr. Brant's speech carries on to examine the degree to which this extension of the ethic of non-interference prevails.

> I was talking to the dentist one day at Moose Factory, [after] he had been examining [a] man. He said [to this man], "I understand that you have some children that I have never seen or examined for tooth decay." The Indian man said "Yes, that's right. I do have a couple of kids." The dentist said, "Why don't you bring them in and I'll examine them and see if their teeth are okay or if they need any attention?" The Native person said, "Yes, I'll see if they want to come."
>
> His children were seven and eight. This Native person was willing to allow his children the choice of whether or not they wanted to go to the dentist. The ethic of non-interference would not allow this man to bring his children kicking and screaming and strap them into the dentist's chair,

because that would be interfering with the child's right to behave as he sees fit. The child may or may not have some appreciation that it is necessary and wise to go to the dentist, but the child will essentially be allowed to make that decision for himself.

Social workers and truant officers are often very annoyed with Native parents who refuse to force their children to go to school. The Native person's response is, "He knows he ought to go to school. What can I do to make him?" *That is to say, how can I maintain my ethic of non-interference and force my child to go to school?* (emphasis added)

When I read that portion of Dr. Brant's presentation, a number of things began to make sense to me for the first time. I, like the social worker and the truant officer, had simply assumed that all people who truly loved their children would take it upon themselves to tell them what to do and how to do it throughout their earliest years, granting freedom of choice gradually as skills and wisdom developed over time. I had assumed that anyone who did not treat their children in that very controlled fashion did not care about them as much as they should. Freedom of choice for an eight-year-old? In my eyes that was tantamount to an abdication of parental responsibility, a sure sign of lack of care.

I began to recall, however, a great many things which seemed to make sense only if viewed from within such a rule. In particular, there was one court case which had stayed as a puzzle in the minds of many people. A young Indian lad had pleaded guilty to breaking into a reserve school at four in the morning with a group of friends, and trashing the teachers' lounge. The judge asked him what his parents had done when they found out about such outrageous behaviour. He replied that they had done nothing. The judge asked if his parents had said anything. Again, the response was a flat no. Angered by this apparent absence of parental concern, the judge turned directly to the boy's father. He asked him if he'd responded in *any* way to his son's intolerable conduct. The father answered that he had hidden the boy's shoes at night.

Hidden the boy's shoes at night? No punishment? No lecturing? No taking him to the teachers for an apology? No offer to have him clean up the mess? To many people in the courtroom, that was as feeble a demonstration of care and concern as could be imagined. It was also such a strange and circuitous response that some people chuckled when they heard it; it seemed almost as if the father was afraid of his boy, as if he wanted to keep him at home without ever letting him know that's what he was doing.

That, of course, was precisely what he was attempting to do, but not out of fear of the boy. Rather, it was out of obedience to the rule against interference in the lives of others, even children, and even for their own good. In his own mind, the father had gone even farther than he should have gone in trying to control his son's behaviour. In our minds, however, he had done virtually nothing. We characterized him as a man possessing only minimal concern, when in fact his concern was so great that it forced him to act against centuries-old commandments. Had we known of his inner struggle, we might well have applauded his idea of shoe-hiding for its inventiveness rather than deriding it. Whether his minimal interference was adequate to keep his son from further harm is one issue; characterizing him as someone largely unconcerned with that future is quite another.

I will later canvass some of the immense difficulties that individual families and entire communities in the North are experiencing in devising child-rearing techniques appropriate to their present reality. Quite apart from the fact that the generation of parents who spent their youth in our residential schools came out of them with no experience whatever of family life to draw upon, today's multi-family, year-round reserve communities are a new phenomenon. They present fundamental challenges to traditional child-rearing approaches, challenges which many communities agree can only be met by the development of new approaches.

For the moment, though, I only wish to underline how perilous it is to judge the motives, goals and desires of people from another culture. Our child care workers, through no fault of their own, regularly see behaviour which, to them, is a clear signal of lack of parental concern. When they see children consistently left to their own devices, apparently free of adult supervision and control, they cannot help but be drawn towards the conclusion that nobody cares. When that conclusion is joined with other culture-specific judgements such as over-crowding (and there is a painful shortage of houses in most communities), the temptation to put the matter before the courts is strong; their duty, after all, requires that they do exactly that when they see a child who, in the words of the legislation, is "in need of protection". If, within the other culture, however, care and concern are demonstrated in different fashions, such a conclusion may well be false.

Ironically, the rule requiring that children be granted immense autonomy may ultimately bring about an opposite result once adulthood is reached: a decision by them *not* to lead an autonomous life. It is Dr. Brant's view that children raised by non-interfering parents become enormously loyal to them and to the entire extended family. They have, after all, enjoyed only pleasurable experiences with them, free of complaint, criticism, advice or coercion. It is unlikely they have found that same sense of freedom in any other context. These children then become, in his words, "layered" onto that extended family. They become integral, as opposed to autonomous, parts of it, and they remain that way for the rest of their lives. While people with my cultural background consciously take steps to promote the successful *departure* of our grown children into wholly autonomous lives (coincidentally freeing ourselves to resume our own pursuits), traditional Native parents aim towards a future where their children will always be around them. In Dr. Brant's words, "We want our children to take over our homes, feed us and support us, etc., even wear our old clothes and ornaments. Thus we will achieve continuity and immortality." There is not simply a different approach to the raising of children at work here but an entirely different conception about the proper role of the family in every person's life. Their family-raising *goals* are, in fact very different from ours. As we shall see in Chapter 9, this goal of maintaining an interdependent or layered family presents Native parents from the remote North with difficult choices when it comes to pursuing educational opportunities for their children. Not only do children have to physically leave for extended periods of time, becoming inevitably immersed in our outside ways; they also find themselves in a system consciously designed to foster an almost complete departure into autonomous adulthood.

✦

The more I thought about the possibility of there being rules against giving advice, even when the other person may be at some risk, the more I remembered incidents from my own experience which, at the time, had puzzled me.

I recalled one day in particular when I was still working as a guide at a fishing lodge and had taken out a group of American fishermen. There were several boats in our party, one of them guided by a Native man and another by his teenage son. The son had chosen to stay a little longer at one spot while the rest of us moved around an island to fish a reef. The rocks on that reef lay just below the surface and stretched out some distance from shore. We positioned our boats around it and resumed fishing. Before long the young lad came around the corner of the island, full throttle, heading directly for the reef. No one, including his father, stood or signalled or yelled to warn him away, though all watched him closely. Surprised by this apparent indifference, I jumped to my feet and yelled at him to cut the motor. He did, but not before the bow of his boat clunked up onto the rocks. There was no damage, but his guests were, as the saying goes, not amused.

For my own part, I wondered how a father could watch his son slide into such a situation and do nothing to warn him. I was drawn to the conclusion that he simply didn't care about his son's safety or reputation, the guests' pleasure or the lodge-owner's property. That conclusion, however, did not fit with what I already knew about that man, for he was a responsible and careful guide who gave every indication of taking pride in what he did. I pushed that incident, unresolved, into a corner of my mind and promptly forgot about it—until Dr. Brant started talking about ethics barring interference in the choices of others.

Brant struck an even more responsive chord when he spoke about the impropriety of giving advice, *even when it is asked for*. As the outside, white stranger coming into remote Native communities to conduct criminal courts, I was always conscious of how little I really knew. For that reason, it was my regular practice to ask people for advice, especially about what kinds of sentence I should recommend to the judge. Just as regularly, I

✦

would be answered by shrugs of the shoulders or "I dunno." On occasion, the response would consist of a rambling story that didn't even mention the events or the people under consideration. Once again, I had the impression that no one cared. At times I felt myself slipping into some sort of vacuum of indifference and non-involvement. I plowed ahead on my own.

I puzzled a long time over Dr. Brant's hypothesis about the impropriety of advice-giving. On several occasions, just to test the hypothesis, I directly asked, "Do you think I should do X?" The response was always something like "Maybe" or "You could". Then I would ask "Do you think I should do Y?" which was exactly the opposite. I usually got the very same response. Quite clearly, the real message was that it was my decision.

I found it impossible, however, to believe that people had no opinions about such issues; I therefore tried a different approach. I did not ask for advice, or even for a recommendation. Instead, I spoke out loud about the various factors which had to be considered in coming to a decision, as if I were only reviewing them for my own benefit. I let the problems pose themselves, without ever directly expressing them. Then I noticed a change. People started to speak. I had to endure long silences, against my every inclination, but I knew that if I jumped in to fill them that the discussion would end. Nothing could be hurried, nor could anyone be interrupted as they too did their thinking out loud.

As I became better at listening, people had more to say. Their contributions generally took a similar form, which amounted to recitations of the various factors involved. On occasion, those recitations would be joined with long stories involving other people, times and places. Over time I began to see that their recitals of fact, often repeated in a different chronological order, as if being chewed over, revealed an emphasis on certain facts rather than others. It was as if the speaker wanted to say that in his or her view those particular facts were more significant than others. Invariably, concentration on those emphasized facts led more towards one sort of conclusion than another. In the beginning, I had to listen hard (and always long!). Frequently I couldn't sort out the meaning of what I'd been told until some time later.

✦

As I began to learn how to listen, two things became clear. First, contrary to my earlier impression, it was obvious that people not only cared a great deal about things but had also given them a great deal of thought. Second, they most certainly held definite views about what the appropriate responses should be. They would not, however, give those views directly. Instead, they would recite and subtly emphasize, often only through repetition, the facts that led towards their preferred conclusion. The listener, of course, had to find that conclusion himself. It became, in that way, his conclusion too.

The same kind of dynamic appears to govern meetings as well. The chairman will never say "Gentlemen, give me your recommendations," and none of the others will say "I think we should do this, and here are my reasons." Instead, everyone takes turns making speeches which recite facts but appear to contain no opinions. One speech follows another, with none of the frequent give-and-take which constitutes a discussion for us. The speeches seem to go in circles, with many things being repeated by each speaker, often more than once. No one seems to venture a recommendation or state a point of view. In fact, meetings often seem to end this way, with no apparent conclusion having been reached at all.

The strange thing is that the participants usually agree that a conclusion *has* been reached. I suspect that this comes about through a process of "distillation" whereby the repetition of certain significant facts in the various speeches leads to a point where there is general agreement on which facts are most significant and only one conclusion seems reasonable. It is as if a common agreement on the pertinent facts which drive a particular conclusion is all that's necessary. The conclusion itself need not even be articulated; everyone goes away knowing what it is.

The only legal parallel I can think of involves trying to decide upon guilt or innocence in an entirely circumstantial case where no one actually saw the crime committed. In a murder case, for instance, there may have been a cigarette butt of the accused's brand found in the dirt of the victim's driveway. He may have been seen in the vicinity close to the time of death. Although his sneakers may have been of a very common type, footprints showing a rough match may have been found outside the forced window. A pack of matches from a tavern frequented by the accused may have been found inside the living room. Death may have been caused from a very deep and narrow puncture wound, and an old-fashioned ice-pick may have been found in the garage. None of those facts alone leads to a conclusion of guilt; taken altogether however, the inference grows strong. At the same time, other facts may give rise to the opposite inference. Perhaps there was no known contact between the accused and the deceased, no motive for the slaying, or a host of other mitigating factors. Deciding upon guilt or innocence requires sifting through all the known facts and distilling them to determine which are the most significant and if, in the end, they prompt a particular conclusion.

It is this sort of ordering of relevant facts, this sort of sifting to shake out the truly significant facts, which I sense governs group decision-making among Native people. The meeting ends and the decision, though perhaps never articulated, is agreeable to all. In this way it becomes a group decision. Most importantly, it is arrived at without anyone "losing", without anyone having his or her opinion ignored or discounted.

When Native people use the phrase "consensus decision-making" I believe they are referring less to the fact that everyone agreed in the end than to the fact that the process of arriving at the decision was communal. It is akin to a process of "joint thinking" as opposed to one where competing conclusions are argued until one prevails.

I have to confess that in the middle of such meetings I can still hear a part of my brain scream "Get to the POINT!" I am gradually coming to the conclusion, however, that any such "point" is far less important in Native eyes than is the process of ensuring that no one feels put down, ignored or "bested" by anyone else. No conclusion at all is preferable to one which is either not supported by all or, worse still, has been arrived at by trampling on the opinion of another participant. No one should feel that he has lost or been forced to give in. Everyone should feel that they have contributed to the decision, that it is "their" decision too.

Behind this rule against advice-giving, then, appears to be a larger rule requiring that no one ever feel bested by another. In the first place, it would be wrong to act as if you were superior in any fashion and, in the second, it would be wrong to make anyone else feel less than adequate. To introduce a theme to be elaborated at length in Chapter 10, the maintenance and nourishment of each individual's self-esteem seems a paramount duty. Anything which might cause another person to lose face, to feel inadequate, foolish or stupid, would be a blow to that self-esteem and an impediment to their development as a human being.

The best illustration of the rule against besting others comes from a story told to me by a Cree Elder from northern Alberta. One day many years ago he and a friend wished to be flown deep into the bush to visit another friend at his trapping shack. They went to a local air service and described the location. The pilot told the manager that he knew where the location was, and they set off. The pilot, however, had only been boasting to his boss. He came within a few miles of the shack (close enough for his passengers to see exactly where it was), circled a few times without seeing it, then returned to base. The Elder and his friend were about to leave without saying a word when the manager asked them directly if they thought his pilot had come close. They assured him that he had. Under further questioning, they acknowledged that they certainly could have guided the pilot down. The manager was both dumbfounded and angry. He assumed that they had remained silent just to show the pilot up, to embarrass him. They, in turn, were equally dumbfounded, because they had kept their silence for exactly the opposite reason. They had not wished to point out, to his face, that his boast had been unfounded and that their knowledge was superior to his.

It is important to note that they would never have raised the pilot's failure on their own. They would rather have wasted their day than offer him such an insult or show themselves in a superior light. When asked directly, however, they felt an obligation to answer honestly. Once again, the cross-cultural conundrum raised its ugly head: they were trying to help the pilot save face and they were accused of doing exactly the opposite. I have no doubt that the Elder and his friend left the office in utter disbelief that the manager could be so rude as to embarrass his own employee in front of strangers. In their eyes, I am sure, it was the *manager* who showed him up.

✦

This care to avoid embarrassing others can be carried to extreme lengths. On one of my court dockets a young girl was charged with a break-and-enter. The duty counsel (a lawyer who accompanies the court party to provide summary advice to anyone who wishes it) told me that he had just spoken to another young girl whom I will call Mary. The police, it seemed, had thought Mary was the accused and had served her with documents, under the name of the accused, requiring her to come to court. Obediently, Mary had come, because that is what the police told her to do. I looked into the file and noticed that the police had taken a statement from someone who had signed the accused's name. That statement denied any involvement in the break-and-enter. I asked the duty counsel who had given that statement, and he replied that Mary had. Why, I asked, did she give a statement and then sign it with the name of the accused? The duty counsel said that he had asked Mary the same question, and that she had answered, "Because that's who the cops thought I was." Rather than tell the police officer, a Native man from her community, that he had confused her with another girl, Mary had given a statement, signed it with the other girl's name, accepted service of a summons and then come to court!

The rule appears to be that it is better to suffer inconvenience and loss yourself than to directly confront someone else with their error. This does not mean that no steps can be taken to correct the error. I suspect that someone who has heard another person say something incorrect will later find a third person who can, in casual conversation, recite the accurate version to the first person. In this way, the mistaken person learns of his error without ever being embarrassed by having the fact of his error drawn directly to his attention. At the same time, no one else ever directly demonstrates superior knowledge.

There is another, much more dangerous aspect to this kind of approach: telling people what you know they want to hear instead of disagreeing with them. Police, lawyers and social workers must be especially wary. If, for instance, you believe you have a pretty good idea what took place and you approach someone expecting them to confirm that idea, that's likely to be exactly what you get, whether or not it happens to be what that person really thinks. Great care must be taken never to ask leading questions to which people can answer "yes" or "no". Instead, questions must be neutral, requiring that all the information come from the person being interviewed. I have seen numerous instances where file summaries indicated that an accused had confessed, but the actual statement amounts instead to an officer giving his version of the event, asking the accused, "Is that right?" and receiving an affirmative answer in reply. When later asked why he confessed to something he did not do, the reply is, "Because that's what the cop wanted me to say." I know that no physical force was used, simply because it wasn't needed; the commandment requiring that you not show up another person by pointing out that he's wrong is strong enough.

I hasten to add that many Native policemen are also guilty of taking statements by using such leading questions, probably because they face the same time constraints that white policemen do and so do not take the substantial time that is required to get Native people to part with full and accurate information on their own. Where the interviewer is an outsider, especially one who works for a potentially threatening agency such as the police or child welfare, people are even more reluctant to give information. It seems to take forever before people will start providing the information officials require, and the temptation to speed things up by putting information to them and then asking if they agree or disagree becomes almost irresistible, though it is, in the long run, self-defeating.

This obligation not to place another person in a position where he is proven wrong to his face is the obverse side of the duty to respect other people's feelings and, if correction is required, to find very gentle ways to accomplish it. Quite obviously, not all Native people still adhere to such cautions. In fact, many of the Native leaders we see on television seem to ignore this rule, hurling criticism and complaint at every opportunity. That does not mean, however, that their behaviour finds favour with the more traditional segments of Native society.

I recall one incident from a conference on aboriginal justice in Alberta sponsored by the Royal Canadian Mounted Police. During the course of a morning workshop a young Native man, a univer-

✦

sity professor, took the floor. He started out by declaring that he was an Elder from a particular band. That declaration startled me, for in my own experience with Elders from remote villages, they seldom state that they consider themselves worthy of that characterization. The professor then went on to detail, with both vehemence and historical accuracy, the terrible treatment his people had suffered at the hands of white people. I agreed with his criticisms but, nevertheless, found myself taken aback by the very direct and confrontational way he made his points. I was used to Elders who were able to make these kinds of points while at the same time keeping everyone present at ease and receptive. At lunchtime another Elder, this one in his seventies and obviously bush-educated, appeared at my side. During the course of the meal he quietly asked if I had listened to the younger one speak. I answered with a simple "Yes", knowing that his question was not an invitation for me to launch into my own critique. He nodded his head and was silent for a long time. I knew enough to wait. Finally he said, "He is a young man yet." In those six words he had, I am certain, offered an apology for the discomfort his brother had caused me. He had also asked me to be patient with him. It was his way of saying that the younger man had not yet learned how to speak with care and respect, but that I shouldn't write him off.

I said nothing in reply, relying instead on a smiling nod of the head and a quiet "um-hmm". I still don't know how to acknowledge a regret or accept an apology properly; I only know that a flood of words is unnecessary. As every Native could tell you (but won't), white men spend too much time talking.

As a footnote, I might add that those six words also spoke volumes about another aspect of Native thinking to be looked at in Chapter 10: the conviction that life is a process of slow and careful self-fulfilment and self-realization. That process of maturation continues until death, and no one ever becomes all that they *can* become. The duty of all people, therefore, is to assist others on their paths, and to be patient when their acts or words demonstrate that there are things still to be learned. The corollary duty is to avoid discouraging people by belittling them in any fashion and so reducing their respect for and faith in themselves. I should

✦

mention that the Elder who reviewed the younger man's performance by saying "He's a young man yet" is the same one who told me the story about the bush pilot who missed the cabin in the bush. In fact, he told the story of that flight at the afternoon workshop that same day, in the presence of the younger man. It is my strong suspicion that it was his way of telling the younger man to always be careful to respect the feelings of the people with whom you are dealing. He smiled at me as he finished it, and I started to have some faith that I might be learning how to listen.

B. THE ETHIC THAT ANGER NOT BE SHOWN

There is another aspect of the behaviour of Native witnesses that has always puzzled me: even when they do choose to speak of traumatic events, there is a flatness to what they say, an absence of emphasis and emotion. Where I would expect to find tears or anger or fear, I instead encounter what appears to be an emotional void.

There are, of course, a number of explanations for this that are not in the least culture-specific. If the violence has been extreme or of long duration, emotional numbness is quite common. In such circumstances people preserve their equilibrium by distancing themselves mentally from the event, with the result that each recitation sounds as if it is being told about a stranger. It is also likely that, for Native witnesses, the impropriety of making critical statements can lead to minimizing or denying certain events, just to avoid further involvement. I began to suspect, however, that there might be other cultural imperatives at work.

Once again, it was Dr. Brant who opened the analytical door for me. In the speech to Native parents from which I quoted earlier, he described a second ethic which he called Anger Must Not be Shown. As before, I'll let him speak for himself.

> This [principle] had its origins in that there were shamans and witches in the bush tribes which [must] not be provoked. They didn't always identify themselves, so it was necessary to be agreeable and not to show one's temper. Also, living cheek by jowl in a tent or a longhouse or an igloo (for the

Eskimo also practice this), anger must not be shown. Restraint of one's angry feelings had to be [practiced]. This also gave, under very close living arrangements, a certain privacy which was otherwise not possible. Your own thoughts and ideas were kept to yourself. . . .

Restraint of anger was a survival tactic in what was, originally, a hostile environment, insofar as it facilitated cohesion of the family, tribe or clan. In other words, the indulgence of personal hostility would have threatened the viability of the group. Thus, as Brant noted, "there was a sacrifice of individual feelings and their expression and discharge for the sake of group unity".

The adaptive function of this rule is not hard to understand, for it parallels what we expect of soldiers in wartime. For the sake of group unity, individual likes and dislikes have to be buried, interpersonal conflicts ignored. It doesn't matter what you think of your fellow soldier because you share a common enemy. In former times, for Natives, that common enemy was the threat of starvation. To ward it off, each isolated, extended family group in the wilderness had to count on the fullest cooperation of all its members. There was simply no room for the playing out of interpersonal antagonisms or jealousies.

The more time I spent in the North, however, the more I came to suspect that it was not just anger which had to be submerged and forgotten. The prohibition seemed to extend to other feelings as well, especially grief and sorrow. These too are emotions which, if indulged, can threaten the group, for they incapacitate the person who is overwhelmed by them. The rule seemed to require that grief and sorrow—and the sources of those incapacitating feelings—had to be forgotten as quickly as possible. Only in that way could the group continue to meet its survival challenges with the fullest attention and energy of every member.

Perhaps the most striking illustration of this approach came from one of the northern reserves in my district where an argument in a newly built and community operated coffee shop escalated into a brawl. One of the participants ended up being killed. Within two weeks, band members had taken chain saws and demolished that new building. Although outsiders could use

✦

the logs and other materials for any purpose, band members could only use them for firewood. It was as if all traces of that disturbing event had to be permanently removed.

A white acquaintance of mine who is married to a Native man told me a story, in a similar vein, about the reactions of her husband's family after one of his young relations died on the reserve. The family quickly removed all of his clothing, possessions and mementoes, and destroyed them. They next removed all the interior walls of the house, then replaced them in a new configuration so that even his room no longer existed. Apparently all family photographs of him were also destroyed, for she related that when relatives came to visit her in Thunder Bay they would quietly, with apparent embarrassment, ask if they could see hers, explaining that theirs were gone. Once again, it was as if all trace of his existence had to be removed so as not to remind people of their loss.

Death is not the only cause for such direct responses. It is not uncommon to find women charged with arson for intentionally burning down their own home. The explanation given often has to do with the fact that the woman has recently discovered that her husband was being unfaithful to her. Burning down the now-defiled matrimonial home not only deprives him of a place to return to, but apparently assists her in forgetting about the life they had together. In traditional times, when the home was a skin tent which the woman built largely on her own, such a reaction was no doubt more acceptable; today's reserve homes are comparatively expensive because everything has to be flown in, so it is understandable that cash-strapped band councils are doing everything they can to discourage such traditional responses.

There seem to be other commandments which involve putting sources of sorrow out of mind. In one community I conducted a preliminary hearing involving a young man charged with throwing his brother out of a boat late one night and leaving him to drown. There had been four people in the boat at the time, and it was important for the court to understand exactly what each person did as the events unfolded. Therefore, my questions were quite specific about each person's acts and words, and I was careful to name them as I went along. The interpreter was from the same

✦

community and it became clear that he was having immense difficulty in phrasing my questions. At a break in the hearing we found out why, for he spoke to the people who had come to watch the hearing. He gave them his apology for having spoken the name of the deceased, explaining that I had left him no choice. To say the dead person's name was clearly wrong to him. I have been told that, indeed, it is wrong to speak the name of a deceased person for a full six months after death, and wrong even to recount stories which involve him for a full year. I believe, however, that it goes even further than that.

I recall prosecuting a young man in another community who, while grossly intoxicated, had driven his parents' car off the road. When it hit the ditch, the car rolled, throwing another young man out the passenger window where he was crushed to death. That happened several years ago. To this day, whenever that event is raised in court as an example of the dangers of drinking and driving, the person who raises it never mentions the dead boy's name or even that there was a death at all. He merely says something like, "We had something happen by the airstrip," or "That morning with the fog and the car."

I refer in particular to an incident in another community, in which a father accompanied his youngest son to court to face a minor charge. I knew that an older son had been killed by a gravel truck several years earlier and that this man had, citing Christian reasons, refused to assist in the prosecution of the driver, who was believed to have been impaired. During the younger son's sentencing, the father again raised the issue of Christian forgiveness. When he addressed the court, all he said about the earlier tragedy was, "Eight years ago this November a gravel truck came down the airport road. I forgave then, and we must all forgive now." He did not mention his older son's name or that he'd been killed.

By that time I was aware of such rules of speaking, and decided to explore them with our interpreter, a well-educated and modern young man from the community. When I referred to what we'd just heard (or *not* heard), and asked about the underlying rule, he just shrugged his shoulders in apparent disinterest. A police officer then asked him if the older son hadn't been the interpreter's roommate when they'd both been out to school. The interpreter replied that they'd been roommates for two full years. At that point someone else came into the conversation, asking the interpreter whom he was talking about. He did not mention the other boy's name, nor did he identify him in terms of his accidental death. He simply answered by saying "The guy I used to room with." He did not talk about the rule, or even acknowledge its existence, but he clearly acted in accordance with it.

I have no idea how many variations there are of this rule requiring that sources of grief not be directly discussed, but it seems to be a fundamental requirement. It also seems to stand in stark contrast to the attitude of determined remembrance which typifies the mainstream culture. Some people go so far as to keep a dead child's room "exactly as it was" for many years. Certainly such things as photographs are regularly protected, and trophies and other mementoes preserved. At the very least, stories of the child's time on earth would not be the subject of a prohibition; in all likelihood they would be recounted with pride.

The prohibition against emotional indulgence appears to be even wider in scope, and to include talking about, or even *thinking* about, one's own confusions and turmoils.

A young Native offender was brought into court one day to be sentenced on a number of serious charges that involved explosions of violence and vandalism while he was intoxicated. It was clear that this young man had many unresolved emotional problems, for he had been constantly in trouble with the law and had already been placed in a number of different institutions. That formed a part of the court's dilemma, for we wanted to find a place that showed the greatest promise of involving him in some successful therapy. We spent a considerable amount of time talking about what he needed when he suddenly interrupted our discussion. He said that he'd been through different kinds of therapy already but that it didn't work. Therapy would fail, he said, not because he was afraid to talk about such things, and not because he was embarrassed to talk about them, but because it wasn't *right* to talk about them. It wasn't right to "burden" other people in that way. Once again, we get a glimpse into a strong conflict between two notions of what is "right".

In the mainstream culture we are virtually bombarded with magazine articles, books and television talk shows telling us how to delve into our psyches, how to explore our deepest griefs and neuroses, how to talk about them, get them out in the open, share them, and so on. At times it seems as if the person who *can't* find a treatable neurosis deep within himself must for that reason alone be really neurotic!

The Native exhortation, however, seems to go in the opposite direction. It is fully consistent with rules against criticism and advice-giving, because it forbids the burdening of others. It is almost as if speaking about your worries puts an obligation on others to both share and respond, an obligation difficult to meet, given the prohibition against offering advice in return.

Even the act of concentrating privately on your feelings seems to be discouraged. Such self-indulgence seems to be viewed as a further source of possible debilitation which poses a threat to the survival of the group.

As a Crown Attorney, I regularly receive psychiatric assessments of Native people in trouble with the law. They invariably say something like, "This Native person refuses to address his psychological difficulties and instead retreats into denial and silence when pressed." Such reports are often full of words like "unresponsive", "undemonstrative", "uncommunicative" and the like. The final word is "uncooperative", with all the negative inferences such a word implies. Of course he refuses to "cooperate", to pour out his innermost thoughts and feelings. For many hundreds of years, that is what his people taught was the proper thing to do.

I suspect that the number of psychiatric mis-diagnoses of Native people must be staggering, for we cannot see their behaviour except through our own eyes, our own notions of propriety. To us, the person who refuses to dig deep within his psyche and then divulge all that he sees is someone with serious psychological problems. At the very least, he is someone who, we conclude, has no interest in coming to grips with his difficulties, no interest in trying to turn his life around. That conclusion leaves the court with long deterrent jail

✦

sentences, rather than rehabilitation, as the only apparent option. I will later consider what kinds of "healing" or rehabilitative measures might be appropriate within Native notions of propriety; for the moment I only wish to underline once again the regularity with which one culture draws negative conclusions about people from another simply because they do not respond in ways we expect. Unable to see beyond our own ways, we fail to see that there are others, and we draw negative conclusions about the "refusal" or "failure" or "inability" of other people to use our mode of behaviour.

There are, then, culture-specific reasons for the refusal of many Native people to enthusiastically recite details of past traumas, how they felt in the course of them or how they are dealing with them in the present. We may be correct when we guess that many Native victims and witnesses do not seem to have even thought about such things, for that may have been their training. It is when we take the next step and conclude that they don't care about such things that we may very well be wrong. How much more reasonable it would be, instead, to ask *them* what steps towards rehabilitation they believe might be helpful.

C. THE ETHIC RESPECTING PRAISE AND GRATITUDE

In the Preface I mentioned learning that the traditionally proper way to show appreciation was to ask the other person to continue with his contribution rather than offer vocal expressions of gratitude. The same sort of prohibition appears to exist with respect to praising the acts of another.

The roots of this commandment, like the others discussed so far, go back to survival times. The harsh environment saw small, family-centred groups fending off starvation in virtual isolation from other groups for most of the year. Each extended family had to perform all the necessary survival tasks itself. Family survival required two things: the best efforts by all, and then the sharing of the products of that effort. Sharing was not, I suspect, what it now is for most of us in this late twentieth-century world, simply a good thing to do. Instead, it was the only thing to do. The same was true as far as putting forth your best effort in all activities.

✦

Not sharing and *not* working hard were quite simply inconceivable. As such, their performance was not a cause for praise or gratitude, save in the most exceptional circumstances.

Dr. Brant concludes, in fact, that sharing and the expectation of both effort and excellence were so central, and so common to Native peoples across Canada, that they deserve joint recognition with the other principles surveyed so far as the dominant ethics of traditional Native life. Without them, that life would have been seriously imperilled.

The expectation of, and obvious need for, excellence in all activities is tied to other attitudes essential in the survival context. Doing something incorrectly, or doing something less productively than it might have been done, could carry disastrous consequences for the group. There was, therefore, a great reluctance to attempt things unless there was a clear likelihood of success. We must remember that, for the most part, this was not a "try-and-try-again" society. Very frequently there would be no second, third or subsequent chances. Resources were simply too scarce to permit much in the way of "practice", and time was often too short to dedicate it to anything but real production.

There seems to be a marked consistency between this attitude of expecting effort and excellence, and the modelling approach to education. If there were neither resources nor time for practice and abstracted "instruction", then the only opportunity for learning would be to watch things being done over and over, in their real-life context, until the child came to thoroughly understand all aspects of a particular task. Preparation involved walking through the exercise in the mind so many times that when the time finally came to act, the young hunter or warrior was doing so in a context with which he was already thoroughly familiar.

D. THE CONSERVATION-WITHDRAWAL TACTIC

This mental-preparation aspect of behaviour—of thinking things through before actually trying them (and refusing to act until the terrain was thus made familiar)—was especially important in situations of stress or danger. Ill-considered or hasty responses

✦

could result in severe harm or death. That rule of the bush is as important today as it ever was. White hunters who find themselves lost often react with a frenzy of activity, losing both energy and presence of mind, sometimes with fatal results. We often react the same way even in situations of minor stress or discomfort: a white stranger at a cocktail party will frequently respond to his discomfort with a frenzy of conversation. If we're stressed, we fall back on action.

The Native response, clearly stemming from survival strategies in the bush, is exactly the opposite. It involves an intentional slowing down to conserve both physical and psychic energy, and to carefully consider all aspects of the new situation before acting. All possible responses are considered, walked through mentally before the commitment to a particular course of conduct is made. For thousands of years this acquired response to unanticipated situations prevailed. That response mechanism, I believe, lingers today, and the greater the unfamiliarity of the new context, the more pronounced will be the withdrawal into physical immobility and silence.

Many Native people, especially youngsters, who are arrested in remote communities and removed to cells in distant centres demonstrate this learned response. A few have been observed to enter into an almost catatonic state and to remain there for days at a time, prompting any number of mis-diagnoses. Native children generally don't do what their white counterparts do. They do not try to instantly dominate their new surroundings, nor do they act up to try to draw attention to themselves. Such responses would obviously have been both futile and dangerous in a hunter-gatherer milieu. Instead, they do as they have learned to do, and retreat into positions of careful observation. We then see, in our jail reports, words like "unresponsive", "sullen", "passive" and the like. The negatives seem to pile up once again, simply because their reactions are not ours. Ironically enough, those Native children who, upon arrival, do act up to call attention to themselves (and their numbers are increasing as satellite television teaches more and more Native youngsters how we behave) are regularly viewed as "normal", and their disruptive responses discounted.

✦

This same kind of response seems to operate in virtually all situations which are felt to be foreign, unfamiliar or threatening, including appearing in court or talking with the newly-appointed child welfare worker. There will be little talking, few decisions, and virtually no commitments to particular courses of action until all the new variables have been carefully examined.

I recall one occasion on which our regular interpreter in a remote village had fallen ill. I approached another man whom I knew to be fluent in both English and Oji-Cree and I requested that he fill in. I offered him the same rate of pay as our regular interpreter. It took an hour before he agreed. During that hour he apparently did nothing more than have a few cigarettes and a cup of coffee, lounging outside on the steps of the band hall where court was to be held. We in the court party, meanwhile, conscious of the length of the docket, grew increasingly frustrated. It may be that he was merely trying to decide whether he wanted to be seen in his village as an ally of the people who come in to take fines and prisoners, but I doubt, from his friendliness, that that was the whole explanation. He was being asked, on the spot, to do something he had never done before. If he agreed to help, especially in such a public role, he needed to be confident he could do it well. I doubt that he was even aware of our frustration, supposing instead that we would appreciate the care he was taking, first in deciding if he was capable of performing his role well and, second, in preparing himself mentally for the task. Once he finally agreed, he acted with both a vigour and a skill which in our eyes completely contradicted the apparent unconcern and lethargy he had demonstrated the endless hour before.

I may possibly have read too much into that one incident, looking for cross-cultural significance in everything I see. I believe, however, that it is far better to look for too much than to see too little. The more time I spend in the North, the more I conclude that there are very few insignificant events when people from different cultures try to interact. To try to turn that interaction into anything that can accurately be called a "meeting" is an uphill battle. It requires constantly anticipating things you've been able to catch only the faintest glimpses of; it is, in the words of my title, like dancing with a ghost.

✦

E. THE NOTION THAT THE TIME MUST BE RIGHT

An attitude complementary to the withdrawal-conservation tactic involves the Native approach to time, more particularly the central (though often misread) notion that "the time must be right."

A people who lived off the land obviously had to wait for the cycles of nature to come round. No one went out to collect blueberries or wild rice or other edibles until they had ripened to the optimal degree. Nor did they trap until the time of year when pelts were at their fullest. And even though some nations were nomadic, to a large extent they had to wait for the large migrations of caribou or buffalo upon which they depended. When they did come, everyone had to be ready. In other words, people had to wait patiently until the time was right, until all the variables came together to provide the best results which were likely to accrue that season. While waiting, they had to prepare their tools and their strategies. Only then would they act, most frequently with immense energy and stamina, for those optimal conditions would not last long. To take full advantage of often short-lived opportunities, each person, and the group as a whole, had to resist acting until the best moment arrived; they had to prepare for activity by walking through the exercise in their minds well in advance, and then they had to perform the tasks with concerted energy and focus.

To introduce a theme which will be looked at extensively in Chapter 6, this mental preparation was critical. The bush is not a grocery store. Animals and plants that provide food and clothing are available in peak condition only at certain times. Each year, each season, and each week will show widely different combinations of conditions, as any sports fisherman can attest. He who fails to anticipate, to adjust, and to strike when conditions are most promising will come home empty-handed. That, in the survival context, could be extremely dangerous.

The notion of "the time being right" is therefore not some mystical or metaphysical construction but a practical, down-to-earth survival tactic. Nor is it a "minor" custom, for it is inextricably bound up with the expectation of excellence and the folly of unconsidered response. It involves not only taking the time to walk through possible courses of action in advance but also preparing

✦

one's self emotionally, and spiritually, for the course chosen. It also requires *not* acting until there is a conviction that the task can be performed successfully.

Nor can we ignore the role that spiritual observance played in preparing for and finding the "right time". Attention to the spirit world required that each person examine their own state of mind before embarking on particular tasks. The butchering of a caribou, for example, required thanking the spirit of that animal for contributing to the family's survival. The task of butchering thus required putting one's mind into the proper state of respectful appreciation. Saying prayers asking for guidance and giving thanks was clearly one of the conscious steps each person had to take to adopt the proper spiritual stance before acting. Until that was done the time could not be right for acting. Successful activity, then, required waiting until all of the physical variables promised optimum opportunity, all the preparatory thought promised optimum performance and, just as importantly, all the preparatory spiritual dedication promised optimal cooperation from the spirit world. Only then could it be said that the time was right for acting with the greatest chance of success.

I think we also have to consider carefully what we mean when we think about "acting successfully". It seems clear that individual success counted for very little, even in the individual's own mind. It was overall success in the enterprise (which had both spiritual and physical dimensions) that was important, for that was what mattered for the group. None of this involved, I suspect, fear of failure as a personal embarrassment. People saw their own importance only in terms of the group, including the group's relations with the spirit world. In fact, they were required to deny themselves the luxury of indulging individual egos. What resulted was a kind of mandatory egalitarianism, supported by all, not only in terms of possessions but in all other respects as well, including criticism, praise, advice-giving, censure and the indulgence of anger, grief or other emotional turmoil. It also resulted in a mandatory posture of gratitude towards and respect for the spirit world which supplied all of life's blessing. Thanksgiving was not an annual ceremony but a philosophical stance which had to be demonstrated throughout each day's activities.

✦

I must admit that my first exposure to meetings with Native people which involved an opening prayer caught me off guard. I didn't feel a connection between the discussion of justice issues (which was the usual purpose of the gathering) and joining in prayer. As I listened closely to both the words and the commitment of the prayer-givers, however, I began to feel differently. Those prayers regularly recite our commonality as human beings struggling to find ways to work towards common goals. They ask for assistance in reminding everyone present of their good fortune to live on such a wonderful planet and with such wonderful gifts. They ask that we remember to treat each other, and the planet, respectfully. I can honestly say that I have been moved many times. I have seen the same reaction from other white people, including bureaucrats, politicians, and hard-bitten policemen. What I sense we are moved towards is a rededication of our minds and spirits. The day's activities will not just involve the *business* of the day's topic, but the *growth* of all people there.

In short, I am beginning to agree with the traditional Native conviction that until each person's mental or spiritual state has been addressed, the time cannot be right to begin the day's particular activity. Minds preoccupied with other issues or full of negative feelings carried over from other contexts will contaminate the proceedings. Those who come to the meeting focused upon individual agendas as opposed to common, larger goals will, consciously or not, put up roadblocks, if only by sending signals of antagonism or defensiveness. By contrast, this simple reminder of the good that is in each of us, of the good that we can each contribute and of the good fortune that surrounds us, prompts real effort at patience, understanding and cooperation.

I am just beginning to understand what it takes for "the time to be right" in traditional eyes, and to see the wisdom of that approach to human activity.

CHAPTER 4

*L*OOKING FOR A SYNTHESIS

All of the ethical commandments touched upon thus far worked together. They were complementary and mutually reinforcing, synthesized into a coherent body of social exhortations that together gave the greatest promise of survival in a harsh environment. If the most basic principles such as non-interference, sharing, and the suppression of disruptive emotions are as different from ours as they seems to be, we can only expect that most others will show a similar degree of difference. My own expectation of difference has done nothing but grow as each new point of divergence has been revealed.

I suggest that we must react differently than we have in the past when we find ourselves puzzled by something a Native person has done or, more importantly, when we are about to come to a negative conclusion about it. Rather than assuming that their behaviour stems from principles similar to ours, and then judging that behaviour badly because it does not conform to our own typical behaviour, we must realize that their behaviour is different because it flows from different basic principles. We are not seeing, despite what we *seem* to be seeing, a people who don't care if their friends make dangerous mistakes or if their loved ones fall into self-destructive habits, who don't care about the peace, health and

◆

security of their communities. We are instead seeing people whose traditional commandments require that they demonstrate their care in two ways which are fundamentally different from our ways: by conferring virtually absolute freedom on everyone and, when damaging events do occur, by doing whatever is possible to put those events behind them, to let bygones be bygones and to restore essential harmony.

Until we realize that Native people have a highly developed, formal, but radically different set of cultural imperatives, we are likely to continue misinterpreting their acts, misperceiving the real problems they face and imposing, through government policies, potentially harmful "remedies".

We also need to realize that these ethics and attitudes are not necessarily seen as "rules" by Native people themselves, just as we are often unaware that vigorous introspection is an acquired cultural trait with us. These sorts of habits represent, to each group respectively, the way they assume all people are naturally. We are seldom conscious of the fact that at some time we *learned* them, and that we could just as easily have learned different approaches instead.

I recall one Native woman at a conference who listened carefully as Dr. Brant spoke about the Ethic of Non-Interference and then discussed some of the problems which that ethic poses for parents trying to raise children in an urban environment. When he completed his remarks, the woman stood up and told us that she had found it very difficult to deal with her children since moving into Kenora from a small northern reserve. Her children were now tempted by friends and activities which she felt could only bring harm, but she had been feeling considerable guilt for stepping in to control them for their own good. She told us that she now understood that her guilt came because she had been brought up with traditional rules requiring that children be left to make their own choices. She went on to say that she felt she could now decide for herself what should be done, and that she would be able to do it with a clearer conscience. Not surprisingly, she had not been aware that her reluctance to interfere had been a learned ethic, or that there were other choices open to her. I have seen identical discussions take place on a number of northern reserves. People there are being forced to examine their traditional rules about raising children now that each extended family no longer lives in isolation deep in the bush.

We must also remember that these learned ethical commandments, though they originated in the survival context of traditional times, will remain in force long after the concern for basic survival has disappeared. Until these commandments reveal themselves to be counter-productive in the changed context of today, they will likely continue to exercise controlling influence. It is extremely difficult to identify such hidden rules and to then begin a conscious assessment of how appropriate they are when circumstances change. It is harder still to see such factors in another person's culture. Instead, we each react with puzzlement to the other's "strange" ways. Unfortunately, neither group seems eager to solve those puzzles; instead, we continue to judge each other by our own notions of what is proper, and inevitably, each concludes that the other falls short.

If I have any one suggestion to make, it is simply this: be alert to any word or act (or *absence* of action) which you are tempted to characterize in negative terms. Ask first whether it evinces some consistency with the kinds of attitudes and approaches which, like non-interference or sublimation, might have been of value in the survival context. There will no doubt be many occasions when condemnation would be the response of *both* cultures, but there will also be a surprising number where your tendency to condemn reflects only your own group's cultural imperatives. For members of the other group, the word or act may have demonstrated the highest allegiance to central ethical commandments.

One horrific example will serve to illustrate what I mean. A psychiatrist practising in Manitoba told me of a very traditional woman in a remote prairie community who looked out her window one day to see her son take a rope, throw it over a tree limb, and begin to tie a noose to hang himself. She called the police immediately, but did not go out to stop him. By the time they arrived, her son was dead. The police later asked Dr. Bruce Sealy (a man whom I will refer to again at the beginning of the next chapter) what they could have done differently. His advice was that they should have immediately ordered the woman, on the telephone, to go out and stop her son. This would have freed her from the grip of her traditional commandment, thus allowing her to do what she so desperately wanted to do.

When we look at this woman's refusal to act in terms of its results, it was a tragic omission on her part. From our cultural standpoint, we condemn her passivity, seeing nothing but a wholesale absence of care and an almost criminal indifference. We characterize her as a value-empty person who ought to be heavily censured. From her cultural point of view, however, the opposite may well be the case. Although her people would no doubt abhor the results of her choice, they would not abhor her. They would not see an uncaring and amoral beast but a woman of such incredible allegiance to centuries-old commandments that she could watch her own son die before breaking them. Whether we agree or disagree with what she chose to do, we must remember that what she *is* constitutes a separate issue altogether. It is possible to respect her as a woman of immense strength and ethical fibre, for in her own culture that is precisely what she proved herself to be. Our response should not be one of condemnation but of sympathetic respect, even though the results of her allegiance were so tragic.

This approach, in my view, is absolutely essential when going into the North, for the central preoccupation of Native people today is with making decisions about which traditional commandments should be carried into the future with full force, which should be modified (and in what ways), and which should be discarded altogether. There may be many instances where allegiance to traditional ways in this late twentieth century produces tragic and (to us, at least) avoidable results. We must be aware both of the magnitude of Natives' struggle, and of the centuries during which traditional commandments proved to be wise and productive. Native people who still follow those commandments deserve our respect as moral, well-intentioned and ethical agents loyal to community-sanctioned precepts. This remains true whether or not their communities decide over time to modify or discard some of those precepts as they take stock of new realities.

✦

It is also important to note that, until fairly recently, Native people across this country have kept a respectful silence about *our* cultural ways, despite the fact that they must have viewed them with considerable alarm, especially when those ways were regularly forced upon them against their will.

We should not forget, for instance, that the people who have represented our culture on northern reserves came from a particular, narrow segment of our society, and that they have, by the very nature of their work, consistently breached many of the traditional ethics discussed thus far. They were, for the most part, what we call "service providers": police, doctors, teachers, social and welfare workers, economic development consultants, alcohol counsellors, lawyers, and judges. Their job descriptions required that they give advice, suggest, cajole, instruct and, on occasion, coerce. In short, they were interventionists, pure and simple. They may have intervened with the best of intentions, but to traditional Native eyes that intention would have been irrelevant. Interference *per se* remains rude, arrogant and wrong. The patience Native people have demonstrated in not criticising us for behaviour they considered repugnant has been nothing short of astounding. Indeed, it is perhaps the clearest illustration possible of their determination to remain faithful to those commandments forbidding criticism of others and the expression of angry thoughts.

It is also clear that at this stage in history Native people are declaring that they have had enough. After putting up politely with our all-encompassing interference for so long, they are asking us to leave them alone, for in many spheres they have seen only negative results.

The court system is one clear example. The function of traditional Native dispute-resolution systems was the real resolution of disputes. They hoped that at the end of their process the parties would be returned to cooperative co-existence, to real interpersonal harmony. Naturally, they expected that our courts would have the same goal. Little did they know that we do not even pretend to that goal. Our society is a society of strangers. Our judicial processes do not aim at restoring friendship or harmony, if only because between strangers these qualities do not exist in the first place. Instead, we aim at deterring harmful *activity* so

✦

that each stranger can continue to follow his private path without interference.

It is little wonder that one Chief recently complained that the court doesn't do what it should do. As he put it, "Your court only comes in here to take money in fines and to take our people out to jail, leaving us with the problem." That problem, needless to say, was the unresolved original dispute between people, or the uncorrected dysfunction within an individual accused. Until recently, Native people have been willing to endure many of the traditionally unethical requirements of our legal system in the belief that we too aimed at restoring interpersonal harmony and individual mental health. That belief was mistaken, for our courts focus primarily on the preservation of public peace. They are concerned not with what people are, but with what they do. The Native approach essentially ignores what was done and concentrates instead upon the personal or interpersonal dysfunctions which caused the problem in the first place. Their first priority lies in trying to correct those dysfunctions rather than in trying to keep those continuing dysfunctions from erupting into further harmful or illegal acts.

It is now the judgement of many bands that our system is inappropriate both in it processes and in its goals. If we are not even going to attempt to do what they believe should be done, they don't want us, for our processes themselves are harmful, involving as they do confrontation and the perpetuation of disruptive issues.

The same sort of dynamic exists with respect to our child-welfare system. Native communities have put up with our interventionist workers in the belief that the fate of their children would be improved. They acquiesced as hundreds of children were taken away and placed in non-Native communities. Many Native children from Manitoba were even placed in the United States. Many such "apprehensions" were based on the strength of our belief that parental refusals to control, coerce and instruct meant a total absence of affection. Native requests that children be placed with grandparents, aunts, sisters or cousins were ignored because the people in charge never understood the cohesiveness, strength, and central importance of extended families.

Now, generations later, Native people have concluded that their children have not benefitted from those placements or, as is more often the case, that they have in fact been harmed in critical ways. Once again, their expectations were not realized and their willingness to go along in contravention of their own notions of propriety has gone unrewarded. They are asking for self government in this area too.

What is remarkable is how infrequently we hear Native leaders say that our system is wrong; instead, they say only that it is wrong for them. True to traditional ethics prohibiting the criticism of others or interference in their choices, they do not pass open judgement on what we do to ourselves, except in the environmental context where they too are equally affected. They do not presume to tell us what to do, as we have told them since first contact. Instead, they are merely asking that they be allowed to devise approaches to their problems which they think are most appropriate. I know that many Native people think our ways of doing things create more problems than they solve, especially that they increase individual anger, alienation, selfishness and envy; they do not, however, wish to be seen as telling us that their way is superior. Instead, they simply assert that "this is our way, ... " and request that we permit them the opportunity to follow it.

This approach, I suggest, is the essence of respect for another culture. I further suggest that Native people have consistently demonstrated this kind of respect for ours. This does not mean that they agree with our way of doing things; they decidedly do not. It means, instead, that they acknowledge our right to make our own decisions about how we think we can best conduct our affairs. They ask for the same in return, and for us to stop denigrating their choices as inferior.

This chapter has proposed attitudes that would help us begin to bridge the huge chasm between white and Native cultures that I referred to in the Preface, by using some of the very principles foundational to Native ethical systems. I don't for a moment suggest that all Native people, even in my small corner of the country, adhere to those principles firmly or at all times. Such is

✦

quite simply not the case. A great many Native people spent their youth in our residential schools, forced to abandon virtually everything from their past in favour of the rigid views of their instructors. Many have been out to university, cut off from their own ways and, in order to succeed, wholly immersed in ours. Many live in close proximity to our towns and cities and have adopted many of our ways. We cannot forget, however, where they started from or the magnitude of adaptation that was required for successful accommodation to our educational and economic systems. What should surprise us is not the degree to which their behaviour may still reflect traditional ways of thinking but how well they have adapted with virtually no help from us. In that connection, we must acknowledge that we have never attempted to fully explain our ways, and that the reason for this failure is that we have yet to acknowledge that a cultural gulf exists at all. At a time when concerted efforts are being made to explore, understand and accommodate the *expected* cultural differences of our Pacific Rim trading partners, for example, such an omission only adds insult to decades of injury.

While the ethics, or rules, discussed so far were clearly aimed towards ensuring physical survival in the hunter-gatherer age (which lasted until well into this century for many Native peoples), I suspect that there also existed a direct synergy with the spiritual beliefs of those times. Native leaders make it clear that spiritual concerns are, and always were, central to Native life. Traditional spiritual perspectives would unavoidably have been integrated with, and supportive of, the behavioral rules already discussed. It is my growing belief, however, that this spiritual dimension may have played more than just a supporting role; spiritual beliefs may have been to some degree *determinative* of those rules.

If rules deal with the proper way of viewing oneself in relation to others, then the concept of "world view" (at least for my purposes here) deals with the proper way of viewing the universe and one's own position within it. Just as we have seen that traditional Native rules of behaviour differ radically from ours in many respects, I suspect we will find that their traditional world view is equally unfamiliar. In a nutshell, I suspect that we have come to

✦

see the universe through what may be called "glasses of science", while Native people have traditionally viewed that same universe through glasses of *super*natural, or spiritual belief.

I appreciate that the following chapter involves a great deal of speculation on my part. I do not believe, however, that we can gain any true appreciation of the cultural gulf which separates whites and Natives unless we try to explore the relationship between traditional ethics and the spiritual view of the universe which accompanied and reinforced them. My speculation may be somewhat off the mark but, as I said at the outset, my purpose is more to raise provocative questions than to provide accurate answers. In any case, I don't think it is open to doubt that in Native approaches to life there is an interplay between the spiritual and physical planes which is central to the individual characteristics of both.

CHAPTER 5

NATURAL SCIENCE VERSUS SUPERNATURAL BELIEF

There are many who share the view that belief in a supernatural order remains an important part of Native culture. Dr. Bruce Sealy, a Métis and a retired lecturer from the University of Manitoba, wrote about it in a booklet entitled *The Education Of Native Peoples In Manitoba*. In a chapter entitled "A Dichotomy Of Views", he raises the issue of what he terms a dichotomy between science and magic.

> In the past, and to a limited extent in some communities today, the world of many Natives had spirits—allies and ene-mies—that were ubiquitous. Magic, ritual, courage and cautious fear allowed them to cope with the world. The non-Native person learns of this and is filled with astonishment, for he has been trained to think of magic as utter nonsense. Science evokes images of objectivity, data collection and accuracy. Magic is thought of as illusions, tricks and sleight of hand. ... Reality is radically different in the two cultures.*

---

*D. Bruce Sealy, *The Education of Native Peoples in Manitoba*, Monographs in Education (Winnipeg: The University of Manitoba, 1980).

How can reality be radically different for two groups when we all possess the same number of senses and deal with the same "things-out-there"? At the risk of offending students of metaphysics, I have my own interpretation of what Dr. Sealy says.

My guess is that the scientific explanation of the universe contains at bottom an assumption that all "things-out-there", or phenomena, owe their activities, if not their very existence, to chains of cause-and-effect. Things are what they are, and do what they do, largely because antecedent things did what they did and were what they were. The assumption posits, further, that if we only design the right tools and approaches we will be able to understand those chains of cause-and-effect. It goes further still, assuming that once those chains are understood and more specialized tools are developed, we will be able to interfere to produce different effects, tailoring them to our own objectives. In short, the scientific view of the universe seems to say that man can, potentially, successfully interfere in everything; man can *control* his surroundings.

In the magical or supernatural explanation of the universe, it is my guess that people believe that things-out-there do *not* owe their existence or their activity to chains of discernible, controllable causes and effects. Instead they believe that those phenomena simply are, and that each acts as it does because that is the will of one of the greater or lesser spirits. There are no "natural" chains of cause-and-effect which can be discerned or altered; there is in each case only a supernatural cause for the way things are and for the way different creatures behave. There is, as a result, little perceived scope for human intervention or control, except through supplication to that spirit world and, in rare cases, through direct intervention by people who wield some portion of its magical power. In most cases, though, one simply accepts that life passes as the spirits ordain.

The degree to which many Native people in the North live within a pantheistic and supernatural view of the universe cannot be over-estimated. Since there may be scepticism about this statement in some quarters, a few illustrations are perhaps in order.

My first acquaintance with Native spiritual beliefs came in 1968 when I was a fishing guide on the Winnipeg River north of

Kenora. One evening a few of the Native guides invited me to their encampment across the river. There they chanted and beat out various rhythms on old oil drums. They were, they explained, calling to the river, asking it to return the bodies of a woman and her infant child drowned several years earlier. There were no feathers, no head-dresses, no moccasins and no tourists; it was not done for show. They were simply addressing the river, beseeching it to respond to their request. I was, quite frankly, floored.

In 1985 I appeared as the Crown Attorney in a Cree community on James Bay. A young woman there had been charged with three counts of shoplifting. She had apparently gone into the local co-op store on three separate occasions and was observed each time putting something inside her jacket, then leaving without paying. I asked why no one had ever stopped her and called a Band Constable. The answer, when I finally found a constable who would tell me, was that this woman's elderly mother practised "bad medicine". People in the community were too frightened of her power to induce physical illness (frequently in forms symptomatically similar to Bell's Palsy) to risk antagonizing her. This conviction gripped a considerable number of people in that village, despite the presence of Anglican and Roman Catholic priests for well over a century.

In a similar vein, an important Crown witness in a criminal trial in Kenora advised the he would not testify against his assailant because that man's family practised bad medicine. Our office ultimately located another man who, the witness agreed, possessed stronger medicine still, but of a good and protective sort. That medicine man was flown to Kenora where he performed certain protective ceremonies, following which our witness appeared to have no difficulty in testifying. (I can report, however, that our Toronto accounting office had considerable difficulty when faced with bills for air fare, hotel and meals which cited "De-Hexing Crown Witness" as the reason for the expenditure!)

I also remember standing on a dock at one northern reserve when a planeload of children came back for the summer from a religious residential school. One young lad carried a bow which he had made over the winter. On it, in pencil, were the words

✦

"God Be With Me In The Hunt". Also on that bow were the pencilled heads of an eagle and of a bear. I knew by that time that the eagle was not an intended target, for eagles occupy a revered place in Native belief. I also guessed that the bear was probably his Clan Spirit, and that both these animals had been drawn on his bow as a supplication. I recounted that incident to some councillors on another reserve a few days later, asking if I had been correct in guessing that by his words and pictures the boy had merely been covering all the bases, paying homage to his Christian God and to his own spirits as well. They all laughed heartily, agreeing that of course that is what he had been doing (and coincidentally chuckling at the fact that his religious instructors, had they known the truth, would not have been pleased). Feeling that I had established a rapport with those men, I decided to explore a little further.

I had read stories of much earlier times on Lake of the Woods south of Kenora.* When Native parents decided that it was time to find their child's Naming Spirit, usually when the child reached the age of eight or so, they would smear the child's face with ashes as a signal to others not to offer food—a necessary warning when children were customarily fed by everyone. In this way, the fasting which accompanied the search for a Naming Spirit began. I asked the councillors who had laughed so heartily with me over the markings on the bow if they were familiar with that practice. They answered that they knew of it, but that like so many other things it had fallen into disuse by the time of their own youth. I then asked, since so many ceremonies and customs had apparently been lost, whether the spirits were still "as strong in each person's heart" as they were in their parents' time.

There was at first a shocked silence, and an atmosphere of what I can only describe as sudden fear. It was quickly followed by a circle of very vehement nods. It was as if even contemplating some lessening of the spirits' power was a dangerous affront. The conversation, light and humorous only moments before, came to

---

*For example, Ruth Landes, *The Ojibway Woman* (New York: W.W. Norton and Company Inc., by arrangement with Columbia University Press, 1971).

a quick halt. I had not only trespassed significantly; I had risked their safety by offering such insult to the spirits.

I did not have the opportunity, therefore, to ask about the rest of the story I had heard about. In it, one young boy asked another who his Naming Spirit was. The words he used, however, were "What spirit are you *not* afraid of?" I had wanted to ask if there were more enemies than allies in the spirit world, but I already seemed to have an answer of sorts: even the friendly spirits could turn dangerous if disrespect was shown.

As chance would have it, around this same time I ran across a telling phrase in a *Time Magazine* article (September 14, 1987) on, of all things, the teaching of writing skills in American schools. It quoted a Sioux student from South Dakota who was writing about his home community: "Life for the Lakota people is going in a downward direction. ... To control it would take great human power or *magic*" (emphasis added).

Anyone familiar with Native people will have his or her own stories of day-to-day events which point not only to continued belief in both good and bad medicine but also in the spiritual plane which makes them both possible. Men and women who practice good medicine and who can, for that reason, teach the old ways are much in demand in Native communities across the country. They spend much of the year travelling and teaching, welcomed wherever they go. Those who continue to practice bad medicine also remain, however, and continue to inspire dread. Early in 1991 people from one community in my district asked for the assistance of a neighbouring community in trying to end, through certain ceremonies, the impact of the bad medicine of someone at home. The spiritual plane clearly continues to play an important part in Native life, despite the fact that many traditional ceremonies were actually banned by our law and virtually all were denigrated as heathen practices. If anything, traditonal ceremonies and practices are making a determined comeback and will once again be a very visible component of daily Native life.

We must be very careful when we consider the role of the spiritual plane. We are not dealing with some quaint custom, nor are we dealing with religion as many of us define that term in our post-industrial, western world. To many Native people, the spiri-

tual plane is not simply a sphere of activity or belief which is sep-
arable from the pragmatics of everyday life; instead, it seems to be
a context from within which most aspects or life are seen, defined
and given significance.

It seems fair to say that when Euro-Canadians think of spirits
we often call to mind Greek or Roman myths, or perhaps the
angels and demons of the Christianized Dark Ages. The former
dealt with the other-worldly exploits of the Goddess of Love, the
God of War, and so on. We no longer see them as independent entities, but as symbols. They have come to represent the often
warring elements of our own personalities; stories of their exploits
seem to stand as metaphorical illustrations of the strengths and
weaknesses we find within our own psyches. In the latter case, we
generally dismiss the beliefs as simply superstitious and gullible.

It is my guess that such was not the case for Native people. I
suspect instead that the spirits were seen as existing quite inde-
pendently of man, and that traditional ethics were to a significant
degree designed to avoid antagonizing those spirits. After all, they
controlled not only the weather but also fish and game, plants,
and even the actions of other men. To a large extent, life was
lived at the mercy of those elements, which meant that it was
lived at the mercy of the spirits which controlled them. If the
spirits chose, they could move through all things-out-there at
will, taking any shape and speaking with any voice.

It is not surprising, therefore, that significant attention had to
be paid to their continual appeasement and pleasure. In this
respect, the text of a letter written by a Father Alneau from an
outpost on Lake of the Woods in 1735 is illustrative of Native
belief—and his own Christianized interpretation of it:

> The devil is the only idol they acknowledge, and it is to
> him they offer their outlandish sacrifices. Some have
> assured me that he has visibly appeared to them. They are
> in great dread of him as, according to their own avowal, he
> is the author of nothing but the evils which befall them. It
> is for this reason that they honour him, while they do not
> give a thought to God, since He sends them nothing but
> blessings. ... When we speak of Christianity to them, one

✦

of their standing reasons for not embracing it is that the Indians were not made for that religion; but the true reason, which they do not wish to avow, is their fear of the devil, and the necessity in which they would be placed of having to renounce what they call their [manuscript indecipherable] which they imagine they could never abandon without being stricken with death.*

The spirits, then, were both powerful and real. They required constant attention. Ignoring their presence was an invitation to disaster at their hands. Given that constant preoccupation, the design of ethics governing behaviour between *people* had to incorporate ethics governing how the spirits were treated as well.

A case in point is the ethic requiring that anger not be shown. Recall Dr. Clare Brant's words: "This had its origin in that there were shamans and witches in the bush tribes which originally could not be provoked, and they didn't always identify themselves, so it was necessary to be agreeable and not to show one's temper." I admit that when I first read that portion of his remarks I paid little attention to the contribution which spiritual belief might have made to the design of interpersonal ethics. I now believe I was wrong in doing so. The "shamans and witches" derived their power from the spirits, with the result that it was necessary to design ethics which guarded against antagonizing both. This ethic then became predominant in dealing with other people as well; one ethic grew to govern behaviour with respect to both planes of existence.

It is likely that a similar dynamic helps explain a phenomenon that all outsiders discuss after working in the North: the degree to which Native people appear simply to accept the ups and downs of life. Where we would rant and rail, they appear to accept hardships and misfortune without rancour or complaint. This stoicism, this apparent passivity and acquiescence, strikes us as singularly odd. Why, we ask, don't they fight?

---

*Rev. Arthur E. Jones, ed., *The Alneau Collection, 1734–1745*, Rare or Unpublished Documents II (St. Mary's, N.S.: Archives of St. Mary's College, 1893).

To be sure, some Native leaders are fighting now, at least against oppression from the outside world. It should be noted, however, that those who lead the fight are often young men and women who have lived large parts of their early lives away from their home reserves, immersed in our Euro-Canadian ways. Although it is seldom seen by outsiders, one of their major struggles involves convincing their own people to join them in standing up to us. This is especially true when they advocate more confrontational or violent tactics, for such directness and overt antagonism are sources of extreme discomfort for many.

Sometimes when we see Native organizations finally coming forward and, in our words, standing up to our governments, we can't help but respond by saying "About time!" In doing so, we express our amazement at the degree to which passivity has seemed to be such a predominant trait. We think of passivity in the face of injustice or oppression as a failing of sorts, a kind of apathy which must be overcome. In fact, this failure to "stand up and be counted," to take action to force change, may flow from a code of ethics which required not forceful response but stoic acceptance, a code constructed upon an underlying belief that it is the spirits which are responsible for things, and that man attempts to force them to change at his mortal peril. Recall again the words of the Sioux boy as he spoke of his people going in a downward direction: "To control it would take great human power or *magic.*"

The pronounced fatalism evident until recently in so many communities may not, in other words, have resulted solely from economic, political and cultural subjugation since contact. That subjugation may instead have been facilitated by a traditionally acquiescent stance towards life's events. If one believes that it is ultimately the spirits who ordain one's fate, whether the immediate causes are weather, harvests, fish, game or the activities of other men, then the entire notion of "fighting back" makes little sense. To do so would, in all likelihood, only further antagonize the very spirits which caused the misfortune in the first place. Instead, the appropriate response involves the "magic, ritual and cautious fear" which Sealy suggests were the traditional methods of coping with the world. Phrased differently, the re-establishment of harmony, health and good fortune on the physical plane

✦

Rupert Ross

♦

depended upon re-establishing as quickly as possible a harmonious relationship with the inhabitants of the spiritual one. It did not involve either complaint or active opposition, and overt antagonism invited only disaster.

Similarly, the ethic requiring the suppression of grief and sorrow takes on a different cast when the spiritual component is considered. If it is the spirits who ordain one's fate, there is simply no point in gnashing one's teeth. Keeping such pain alive not only threatens survival by reducing energy, will power and attention; it is also pointless, because the initial tragedy could not have been averted. Misfortune had to be accepted, then put behind as quickly as possible.

When misfortune comes not through illness, accident, weather and the like, but through the acts of other men, this exhortation to forget takes on a different significance. Those who work in the North are regularly astounded by the extent to which Native people routinely welcome back into their midst people who have done them significant harm. Most communities stand behind those people and regularly ask the court not to take them out to jail in the first place. Even when they agree that a particular offender has to go out because of the risk he poses to the safety of others, they appear to be almost entirely without rancour or blame. On the contrary, there are often demonstrations of heartfelt regret, as if they are sorry that things went so far wrong that no other option remains.

It is not unusual to see the families of victims line up after court to give a hug and farewell handshake to the person who victimized them. Just recently, I watched that phenomenon occur again, but this time in a somewhat surprising context. A young man had severely beaten his wife in an alcoholic rage, breaking her jaw with punches as he held her to the floor with a knee on her neck. The community leaders (all of whom were male) spoke of the young man's sincere efforts to deal with his alcohol and anger-control problems. They advised that he had not touched alcohol since the night of the assault, that he had been of great help to his family and that he felt very strong shame about his acts. They asked that we not take him to jail, preferring that he remain in the community so they could continue to assist him as he tried to

♦

58

change his life. It was my position, accepted by the judge, that such a beating required a jail term if only to send a message to other men that they could not permit their anger to express itself in physical violence. The judge spoke at length about the Elders' role in assisting individuals such as the accused and his wife to settle their problems and, if possible, to return to a harmonious relationship with each other. He did his best to explain that the court had a duty which extended beyond the particular man and woman involved in any one charge, a duty to do what it could to protect other women by warning men that they would be punished if they gave in to physical violence. The courtroom was jammed, and there were a large number of women there.

After the young man was sentenced to jail, he was escorted outside by the court officer. They then had to wait before boarding the police plane while family members rushed home to collect some things for his trip out. As they waited, they were slowly surrounded by a small crowd of about fifteen people, *all of whom were women*, most of whom were elderly. They kissed the offender and whispered in his ear. There were some quiet tears, a couple of photographs were shyly taken, and then he was led away. There was absolutely no sentiment of "he got what he deserved" or "good riddance".

I stood watching that scene, as I have watched others, wondering what all those hugs and kisses meant. Did they mean that the women opposed what was happening to him, that they felt no sympathy whatever for my arguments about trying to protect them from the physical abuse of their men? Was I simply one of the bad guys from outside who had no understanding of proper behaviour? I must admit to having those kinds of thoughts and to feeling that I was one of the least-liked people around.

One possible interpretation of their demonstration of affection for the young man, one which contains no necessary condemnation of either my position or the judge's decision, has been alluded to in earlier chapters. Each of those ladies knew that when his jail term was over he would come back. If he came back feeling reviled by the women of the village, his problems with women would only grow worse. If, in contrast, they demonstrated their forgiveness, their support and their waiting welcome, the opposite result might occur. In their view, while jail sentences might on occasion be necessary for the protection of all, the person who has to pay that price should not be cut off from community affection and support. To do so would only put the community further at risk. Just as importantly, it would be an abdication of the group's responsibility to nurture and support each of its members, in good times and in bad, and especially when their need to feel valued was greatest. I have no doubt that they made a very strong impression on the young man. (I must admit to having no explanation for the fact that no *men* gathered around him or came to shake his hand; they seemed instead to keep a careful distance.)

For many years I have watched such demonstrations, marvelling at what appears to be an extraordinary capacity for forgiveness. I am aware that there are very practical reasons in tiny communities for people not to antagonize dangerous persons who will someday come back. In traditional times, of course, even dangerous psychopaths might be needed if it came to war; keeping them around and on side might well pay future dividends. I do not, however, believe that self-interest constitutes the entire explanation. Nor do I think that such demonstrations of affection come entirely from rules requiring that people sublimate anger for the sake of maintaining the greatest group capacity for survival, just as soldiers in wartime are required to put aside interpersonal hostilities in the face of a greater common enemy. What has constantly amazed me in such circumstances is an apparent absence of rancour, the maintenance of what I can only call real affection.

I am not as certain, however, that this maintenance of affection is synonymous with forgiveness, at least as I understand the concept. My hypothesis is, instead, that what we are tempted to call forgiveness is in fact something substantially different, and that it is related very closely to their spiritual world view.

The critical difference, in my view, has to do with the concept of blame. Forgiveness, to me, involves an initial supposition which I am not certain I see among Native people in the North: the supposition that the other person could have avoided his harmful act in the first place. What makes forgiveness difficult in

✦

normal circumstances is the underlying conviction that the damage could have, and should have, been avoided if only the person
had been more restrained, more temperate, more thoughtful, more
careful. If, by contrast, the basic conviction is that people behave
as they do because they are to varying degrees the instruments of
outside forces, the entire issue of forgiveness poses much less of a
problem. To use our expression, it would be inappropriate to
"shoot the messenger", simply because the messenger is not to
blame.

If, for instance, our one-year-old child breaks a dish, does the
issue of forgiveness really arise? Do we blame the child in the
first place? Do we hold him or her *responsible* for what they've
done? Or do we instead come to the instant conclusion that it
wasn't the child's fault, and then simply do our best to forget
about our loss. I suspect most of us do the latter. We conclude
that the child was not responsible, that no blame can be attached,
and that as a result the entire issue of forgiveness does not arise.
If, by contrast, one of our teenagers breaks a dish, different consid-
erations come into play. We probably hold them responsible; we
see an element of personal fault in their behaviour and attach a
degree of blame. At that point the issue of forgiveness indeed aris-
es, together with a consideration of punishment as a means of
deterring repetition of the act. The more intentional, repetitious
or serious the misbehaviour, the more we consider escalating the
punishment. At the same time, real forgiveness becomes increasingly difficult.

This sort of response, however, does not seem to occur in the
majority of Native communities with which I am familiar, nor
does it seem to be a response which comes naturally to the people
who live there. It is the notion of *blame* which seems to be missing. By way of illustration, I would like to quote from a proposal
made to the Ontario government by the Sandy Lake Band of
northwestern Ontario. They wished to secure funding for various
justice initiatives, including the selection of community Elders to
sit with the court and make recommendations when it came time
to pass sentence on offenders. In their proposal they addressed
some of the things which they felt created problems when the
outside court system dealt with their people.

✦

Probably one of the most serious gaps in the system is the different perception of wrongdoing and how to treat it. In the non-Native society, committing a crime seems to mean that the individual is a bad person and must be punished. ... The Indian communities view wrongdoing as a misbehaviour which requires teaching, or an illness which requires healing.

I will return to that quotation in Chapter 10 when I examine the Native notion of "healing" and their sense of what a person really is. For the moment I wish only to point out their conviction that our two societies operate under very different perceptions of the causes of social misbehaviour and of the responses which might be most appropriate. Native communities regularly oppose jail; indeed, they oppose anything that appears to have no function other than punishment. Instead, they focus on teaching and on counselling, together with compensation or resitution where suitable. They are most reluctant to conclude that an individual can no longer benefit from their efforts. When they are finally forced to conclude that an individual poses too great a threat for the community to live with and must be removed, it is quite clearly a conclusion of last resort, and it is announced with real regret. They will regularly tolerate degrees and frequencies of criminal misbehaviour which in our eyes seem extreme.

The apparent inappropriateness of the concept of blame is, I have come to believe, likely a product of many forces, all of them mutually supporting and strongly interrelated. One of those forces, perhaps even a major one, is a belief system centred on the existence of a vast number of spirits which regularly influence the affairs of man. I emphasize that it is only a contributing *part* of the explanation; a search for the other contributing parts must wait until Chapter 10, where I attempt to tie all of the individual explorations together.

In essence, then, the traditional belief system holds that it is the spirit world which ordains one's fate. The disapproval of punishment and the readiness with which Native people welcome back even dangerous people lead me to suspect that they operate under a very different notion of human responsibility. So too does their reluctance to criticise anyone or even to think critical thoughts. By the same token, the almost complete absence of expressions of praise seems to reinforce the hypothesis; why would you praise a man unless you believed that he personally overcame some obstacle or strong disinclination to take the action that he did? Praise and gratitude appear to me to be instruments we employ to prompt people to continue making the kinds of choices they do, just as censure and punishment are instruments used to stop people from acting as they have. If, however, the underlying conviction is that it is one's interaction with the spirit world which largely determines such choices, then notions such as praise and blame or reward and punishment no longer make sense. The appropriate responses involve teaching people how to rid themselves of spiritual contamination and how to avoid contact with it in the first place.

The Ojibway word which is used to denote their notion of forgiveness is "aubwaewaenimauh", which I have been told means, in its most fundamental sense, either "to release a person from ill will", or "to thaw one's cold antipathy towards another". Implicit in at least the first translation is the notion that the feelings of one person can in some fashion reach out and encumber another. Forgiving involves getting rid of that feeling within your own heart, which then has the direct result of freeing the other.

Recall, in this connection, Charlie Fisher's description of the purpose of the Elders representing the two disputants in traditional times. Their role, he said, was to assist each person to "rid himself of his bad feelings". When I first heard him, I thought he was referring to personal feelings like anger or jealousy which, we all agree, must be brought under control. I now believe that he was not talking about feelings internal to each person but about negative influences which had, in some sense, invaded the person's "soul" from without. The spirits within you could in turn reach out from you, or through you, to affect others. In other words (and using *our* words) he may not have been talking about self-analysis and self-manipulation as we understand those terms, but about something akin to exorcism.

Charlie Fisher also said that if the Elders' counselling was successful, each person would be "cleansed" and "made whole again". The final result would be that each party was "restored to himself and to the community". Too much significance can, of course, be placed on the use of such phrases. This is especially true where the challenge is to use one culture's words to describe another culture's concepts; if we lack the concept it is unlikely we have ever fashioned the words necessary to convey it accurately. The apparent consistency between all the various indices, however, seems compelling: no punishment and no praise; no expressed criticism and no expressed gratitude; the requirement that turmoil be forgotten; no allocation of responsibility and no imposition of consequences. Instead, the emphasis is entirely upon healing and upon teaching. All of these things, when coupled with the known importance of supplication to and appeasement of the spiritual plane, point strongly towards a very different view both of human choice and human responsibility.

As believers in chains of cause-and-effect, we tend to punish or reward in the hope of causing certain choices to be made. As believers in supernatural causes of daily events, at least in traditional times, Native people may never have considered punishment. If all human beings (and, for that matter, fish, animals, plants, and all natural objects) were seen not as independent entities but as instruments employed by the spirits to implement their will, then punishing each other would constitute an empty act of viciousness serving no purpose whatever.

On occasion I have initiated discussions in the North which at least skirted this issue (remembering that, for the most part, discussion of the spirits' power is regarded as improper, if not dangerous). One day I met with the Chief and council of a fairly large reserve to discuss justice issues. I decided to approach things from a philosophical, instead of technical, point of view. I explained why we chose jail and fines as responses to criminal misbehaviour, outlining our view that such responses might prompt people to make different choices in the future. When the translator completed my explanation, there was what I can only describe as an excited but incredulous outburst of comment from around the table. One Elder exclaimed, "So that's why you do it!"

I think I was more dumbfounded than they were. I had no idea that a system of deterrence would be such an apparently foreign notion to them. Similarly, I was more than a little surprised to

✦

find that they had permitted our courts to come in for so many years without ever arriving at a clear understanding of why we did the kinds of things we did. In turn, I think it is fair to say that we had never come to a clear understanding of why they so regularly opposed our responses of jail or fines. I began to see why, in earlier meetings with them, I had seen only puzzled stares when I asked what they did to people who broke community standards before the court came. The answer was that they did nothing *to* such people; they counselled them instead.

A belief system centred on a spiritual plane interactive with the physical one cannot help but give rise to different approaches to other kinds of issues as well. If the universe is seen as largely controlled by independent spirits over whom man has only limited power, active interference in the workings of that universe runs the risk of offending those spirits. The appropriate attitude would be one of extreme circumspection, taking care to cause as little distrubance as possible on either plane. If, by contrast, the universe is seen as nothing more than a gigantic web of cause-and-effect relationships, then an opposite philosophical stance might well seem appropriate. Interference in and manipulation of those causal relationships to suit our own purposes would come to represent initiative and progress. Learning to alter and control things for our own benefit would be seen not so much as a dangerous affront but as a virtual duty.

Attitudes as different as these could not help but colour a great many things for both groups. Euro-Canadian society has come to prize as virtues aggressiveness and a dogged determination to prevail regardless of the odds. Native people, by contrast, value quiet accommodation instead. One group sees itself as properly the master of all creation; the other as a component and dependent *part* of all creation. In turn, the two groups cannot help but characterize each other in negative terms: we decry their caution and passivity as apathy, while they see our aggressiveness as arrogant and willfully wrong.

It seems, then, that a number of the cultural differences between us are attributable, at least in part, to this distinction between a scientific and a supernatural view of the universe. Once either view is adopted, attitudes towards things-out-there

✦

cannot help but form differently. In turn, different approaches are developed for the "proper" way to relate to each other, to one's own fate, and to the natural surroundings. All such attitudes and approaches are of necessity mutually supporting, interconnected and interdependent. Our task, if we wish to achieve real communication, is to learn as much as we can about the other's world view.

Before concluding this chapter, I feel compelled to address another issue: the degree to which our much-heralded science may be on the verge of telling us that many traditional Native convictions about the right way to behave towards thing-out-there may indeed be necessary for the survival of all societies on this small planet.

I don't mean to suggest that western science is ready to argue for the resurrection of a spiritual plane full of god-like entities ready to punish arrogance and reward humility. I mean instead that science may be warning us that we cannot continue our massive interference with the natural equilibria without having that interference come back to haunt us in very concrete and life-threatening ways. It may be telling us that we are indeed dependent upon harmony within the ecosystems which both surround and nourish us, and that the destruction of that harmony can only result in our own destruction as well. It may be telling us that Native attitudes like accommodation and respect must quickly replace those of mastery and manipulation. In other words, I find myself wondering if Native conclusions will not be proven correct, regardless of how they formed.

In a sense, it seems as if certain attitudes may be coming round full circle. There was a time in our history when our forebears too looked about themselves to see a pantheistic world full of watchful and meddling spirits. In the works of Homer, we find his heroes making supplication to one god or another on virtually every page. Students of the Greek tragedians will recall a gradual change until, by the time of Euripides, his characters were praying that certain aspects of their own natures would prevail over others; the real struggles were seen as occurring not upon Mount Olympus but deep within each person's psyche. This was also the

✦

era in which "modern" science was born, though the scientists of the day were, even in their own minds, simply philosophers. Such thinkers as Aristotle postulated the existence of laws of cause and effect as determinative of events, and these arguments slowly contributed to the weakening of belief in other-worldly causes. The birth of natural science required, and saw, the erosion of a supernatural conviction.

Our mechanistic, cause-and-effect science has permitted an astounding degree of interference in the natural order. At this time in history, however, it is also beginning to tell us something else: there are heavy prices to pay. In that sense, our science, our very tool of interference and control, is itself sounding a warning about its own limits. We appear, for instance, to be on the verge of "discovering" that many varieties of antisocial behaviour may be caused, in ways not yet understood, by external influences such as high lead levels in air or water. Similarly, our social scientists are warning us that children who grow up in assaultive homes *learn* that behaviour and are to a large extent destined to repeat it in their own adult lives. Suggestions of this sort may well come to challenge our belief in individual free choice and responsibility to a significant degree. If that occurs, we may well have to reconsider our reliance upon punishment, and instead focus on both healing and *un*-learning, or teaching, just as the Sandy Lake Band described it in their justice proposal.

In short, we may find that our sciences, the supposed antithesis of Native spiritual belief, may be telling us things that sound strikingly similar to Native commandments. In particular, they may inform us that we must modify our insistence upon manipulation and mastery in the direction of accommodation and respect. If that is the case, if we begin to change our attitudes about how to treat the natural order, will we in time find ourselves leaning towards ethics of non-interference and respect when dealing with people too? How closely are such attitudes interconnected?

Whatever the answers may be to this kind of question, it seems clear that at least until this point in history the Native and non-Native world views have been distinctly at odds with each other. Because we have viewed the universe so differently, we

◆

have each developed different notions about the proper way to deal with the natural order, with each other, and with ourselves. It also seems clear, however, that both world views are presently in a state of flux. Native people want to become involved in and share the benefits of our scientific progress and, perhaps, to escape the varying degrees of tyranny which certain aspects of the supernatural plane imposed. Many of us, on the other hand, are beginning to realize that our arrogant assertion of independence from and mastery over the natural order may yet be our ruin. At the same time, I sense that many of us are beginning to wonder if our single-minded pursuit of material advantage, coupled with substantial neglect of the spiritual side of existence, won't leave us in the end feeling substantially impoverished.

In that respect, I find myself wondering, with increasing frequency, why Native and non-Native people have yet to recognize and acknowledge that it would be profitable for all if we could listen to and come to an understanding of the other's perspectives.

In the exploration thus far I have tried to examine traditional Native ethics or rules concerning the proper way to approach the universe, other people and one's own mental or spiritual health. I then suggested the possibility that such ethics were, if not determined by belief in a spiritual plane, they were at least shaped in full conformity with attitudes fostered by that belief.

I now wish to go one step further. I want to explore the possibility that everything discussed so far was itself caused by something more fundamental still: the unique way the mind must work when the task at hand is survival in a hunter-gatherer context. I undertake this exploration not simply as an academic exercise. I strongly sense that once the mind becomes adept at that unique kind of thinking it will inevitably be drawn towards the kinds of ethical and spiritual conclusions discussed so far.

At the same time, it is my conviction that we can never truly apprehend the real texture or significance of those ethics and spiritual beliefs until we gain some glimpse of their origins. In a very significant way, the discussion thus far about the spiritual plane was misleading, for, as one correspondent phrased it, it appears to perpetuate the notion "that Indians believe little spirits live in trees, rocks and waterfalls". A more complex and, I hope, accurate

✦

look at the content of spiritual belief had to await the discussion which follows. As I indicated in the Preface, the wholeness of Native reality is indeed greater than the sum of its parts. But, equally true, the parts themselves cannot be fully seen until the shape of the whole is known. Until we see how the survival context dictated a certain kind of thinking, the results of that thinking (whether they be pantheism, ethics of non-interference, a modelling approach to education, and so on) will remain, for the most part, unconnected cultural idiosyncrasies whose full force cannot be appreciated.

If I have one strong conviction about Native people in traditional survival times, it is that they lived *in their minds* to a much greater extent than we have ever imagined. At the same time, those minds were required to operate in a fashion which we seldom employ. That, then, is the enterprise of Chapter 6: a search for the very cast of mind which created what we have explored thus far.

"BEING INDIAN IS A STATE OF MIND"*

Traditional rules of ethical conduct and traditional views of a spirit-dominated universe did not come into being on their own. They were created. The context of that creation was survival by small family groups alone in the wilderness. We can see how they make sense in that context, but I think that their origins go much deeper than sheer utility. I suspect that they owe their creation to the fact that survival in such a setting required the human mind to operate in a unique way, one that is very different from the way that prevails in our post-industrial world.

The hunter-gatherer did his shopping in the natural world. As already noted, his success depended upon his ability to accurately read the innumerable variables which each season, day and hour presented. Those variables, however, presented patterns which, over time and with great attention, one could learn to recognize. Reading those patterns to determine when "the time was right" was the essential life skill, and it constituted, in my view, a very specialized form of thought. For the sake of convenience, I will call this way of thinking pattern-thought.

---

*This expression was used by Gary Farmer, a Native actor, in an interview with the Toronto *Globe and Mail* newspaper, April 22, 1989, p. C1.

◆

My own glimpse of this other way of thinking came from my eleven years as a fishing guide, the closest I will probably get to sharing the hunter-gatherer experience. I obviously possessed nothing close to the observational skills of the Native hunter, nor could I pretend to share his ability to use those observations to draw conclusions about what course of action might be most promising. My very limited observational skills permitted me to read only the most blatant signs and signals, and the foreignness of the thought process permitted me only the crudest form of "native" reasoning. I am satisfied, however, that I began to develop the rough dynamics of that other way of reasoning. It took years, and I still have a very difficult time trying to describe the process involved.

As a guide, my job was to find where the fish were actually feeding. When I started, the more experienced guides provided opening pointers. Our quarry, pickerel (which our American guests called "walleye"), formed into schools and, as the water warmed over the course of the summer, those schools moved gradually into cooler, deeper water to maintain a constant body temperature. When they did so, they moved en masse to new locations to keep similar kinds of bottom structure around them at the new depth. The result was that at any given time of year there might be twenty different schools at twenty different locations around the lake. At some time during each day, each of those schools would spend an hour or so feeding. The trick lay in being there when they did.

On each day, therefore, the other guides would provide me with a list of twenty spots that might prove profitable. For me, the problem came in trying to decide which of those twenty I should try first, second, third and so on. It was at this point that no one could provide any assistance whatever. The experienced guides, however, inevitably did well, usually visiting only five or six of those spots while I frantically canvassed all twenty. When I asked why they chose the spots they did, no one could explain except by saying, "I played a hunch," or, "I just had a good feeling about those spots." Their consistent success, however, strongly suggested that more than "feelings" or "hunches" were at work.

In time, I too began to get "feelings" about where to go, "hunches" about what spots would produce feeding fish. As the years passed, those feelings became more and more reliable. I believe now that I was developing a different form of reasoning. It seemed largely subconscious then, and even today there are aspects of it which resist clear explanation. As best I can describe it, the process went something like this.

Before collecting my guests and heading off for the day, I spent some time on the dock trying to get a "feel" for the day. I made mental notes about such things as wind speed and direction, cloud cover, temperature, and so forth. Over time I began to make more subtle observations. I began to incorporate things like the quality of the light, the humidity, the sense of disturbance-building or disturbance-waning. In truth, I simply cannot list all of the things that were finally incorporated into this "feel" for the day. I don't believe that they ever came to my conscious attention, but they were noticed all the same.

The next step involved taking that general "feel" for the day and, if you will, superimposing it mentally on each of the twenty candidate spots. It was an attempt to imagine what each of them would feel like were I actually to go there. Gradually it became much more than just imagining them; they could almost be experienced well in advance of going there. For want of a better term, I'll refer to this process as one of "imaging" those spots.

A very large number of variables went into that imaging process. Many, like strength of wind, were incorporated consciously, for the same wind could produce high waves in one exposed location and only swirling "cats-paws" in a protected one. Similarly, an early morning sun would leave some shorelines in shadow while others would be brightly lit. In areas of strong current, the colder bottom water would be swirled to the surface to keep the air cool, while shallow bays of unmoving, sun-soaked water would keep the air above them warm. That list of variables was only limited by my capacity to observe. Similarly, the accuracy of my imaging was limited only by my experience, by the frequency with which I had actually gone to those spots and compared the reality with my expectations. As the years went by, my capacity to accurately image remote spots grew to the point where I could get a pretty good feel for them well before leaving the dock; there were fewer and fewer surprises when I actually went to try them.

✦

It is the next step which is the hardest to explain. It is the step at which certain of the twenty spots seemed to attract me as I stood on the dock, to draw me to them, while others left me cold. This process seemed to happen very quickly and without conscious effort on my part.

I can make this step intelligible only by thinking of my dock image of a particular spot as a transparency of sorts, with all the variables sketched opaquely on its surface. Then similar images of past days at the same spot are slid under it. What I look for, of course, is correspondence between what I anticipate and what I recall. The operating assumption is that the greater the degree of correspondence between the feel of today and the feel of an earlier day, then the greater the likelihood that what happened then will be repeated now.

These memory images of earlier days, however, seem to present themselves in an order of their own, an order which I think is based on their emotional force and content. An earlier day of tremendous fishing will come with a strong emotional force and a very positive content. An earlier day of absolute failure will come with comparable force but with a negative emotional content. The stronger the emotional force, whether positive or negative, the more likely it is that those memory images will be the first to present themselves.

I must stress this issue of emotional force, for what seems to take place is not just a simple recollection of an earlier day, but a virtual recreation of the feelings experienced then. In a way, it is comparable to the phenomenon of a man re-experiencing the intense yearning of his youth when he meets someone wearing his first girlfriend's brand of perfume; he doesn't just remember what he felt like then, his heart aches all over again. Standing on the dock, being presented with these memory images of past days, I would assess degrees of correspondence and review emotional content. If there was a marked correspondence and the emotional content was both strong and positive, it would *feel* like a good spot to try. If there was only a vague correspondence but strong and positive emotional content, I might feel that spot as a long shot. If there was no correspondence, there would be no feeling at all about that spot.

✦

The peculiar thing about this process is that it did not take place consciously. I could neither follow it nor describe it step by step to others. When I finally came to conclusions about what spots I would go to first, those conclusions appeared not as logical deductions but as emotionally charged sets of expectations: "Spot X feels hot today!"

What was taking place was, without doubt, a very complex and compacted form of reasoning. We are tempted, however, to deny it that status. In the first place, it emerges with an emotional content we see as foreign to "pure" or rational thought. In the second, its conclusions do not admit of reasoned back-tracking or explanation. The reasoner himself is unable to report his reasoning process. Even if he were able to make out a complete list and then describe all of the variables in each memory and dock image, it is highly unlikely he would be able to trace and then explain all of the points of correspondence and divergence between the two patterns which led him to his ultimate conclusion. In fact, it is almost as if conclusions create themselves, then announce their arrival with an emotional "There!"

I know that this was always the case when I asked other guides why they had chosen the spots they did, and I was no better able to explain my own selections when I too began to enjoy some success. Try as I might, the best I could say was, "It felt right," or, "I caught fish there before on a day like this." When pressed to explain what I meant by "a day like this", I could never produce a catalogue of things coming anywhere close to my total sense of the day; there was no way I could describe their sum. Some spots just felt good, while others did not.

I believe it was this sort of mental process that guided the choices of the hunter-gatherer. His central daily, unending preoccupation was with this one mental task: accurate prediction. Successful prediction could not, of course, be accomplished without paying close attention to details and to patterns, but that was not enough on its own. Observational skills had to be accompanied by a storing of those patterns in memory and by a skill at comparing those stored patterns, in their incredible diversity, with the ever-changing patterns of the day at hand. As experience increased, so too did the wealth of stored patterns, making it

increasingly likely that a "match" could be found for any succeeding day. At the same time, increased experience would enable
each person to "see" more each day, to absorb more detail and
discern ever more subtle patterns. In the same way, an experienced deer hunter will spot many more deer with his trained eye
than a novice will, even though the two of them stand side by
side with equally good eyes trained on the same hillside. Time
alone permits a sharpening of these skills of perception.

I can recall one particular day when I realized that my own
perception skills had shifted onto a new level. I was guiding a
man and his young son one beautiful August morning. We were
some twenty miles from camp, fishing the very exposed north
shore of a large body of open water. The sun was shining, there
wasn't a cloud in the sky and the light southwest breeze gave us
the small waves that are perfect for walleye fishing. The fish were
biting, and all was as it should be.

Around eleven o'clock, however, I began to feel uneasy. That
particular shore is a dangerous place to be if a storm comes up
from the south, for there is little shelter and lots of room for
heavy waves to build. Over the next half hour or so I watched the
sky carefully for any signs of change to justify my concern, but
there were none. Still, my uneasiness grew, my sense that something was coming. I finally told my guests that the air "didn't feel
right" and that we had better get ourselves back across the open
water to the south, into the shelter of a string of islands.

They were not happy, for the fish were biting and, as I readily
conceded, there was no visible threat on any horizon. I was insistent, however, and they reluctantly reeled in.

It took us over half an hour to cross the open water, and during that time nothing visible changed. The sky was still
absolutely clear and the breeze remained light. When we stopped
to fish on the north side of an island I again took stock of things.
The air "felt" worse still. After half an hour (with no bites, I
should add), I suggested we head still closer to camp. It is accurate
to say that my guests were becoming increasingly grumpy, convinced that they had a guide who was determined to be in early.

When we rounded that island and broke into the channel
heading south, their unhappiness turned quickly into fear. Ahead

✦

of us was the most threatening storm cloud I had ever seen. Its leading edges curled up high and then back in towards the centre, and it was green and black in colour. It was not large, but it completely blocked our route home. I headed back to the north side of the island and pulled the boat in close under a large cliff. We waited there for about fifteen minutes. During that time we felt the temperature drop a good twenty degrees. The storm cloud carried its own winds, and when they raced up the channel they churned the water into large, white-capped waves advancing in a solid front. Within minutes we were battered by quarter-inch hailstones that forced us to put our seat-cushions over our heads. The storm only lasted some fifteen minutes, then left us once again under the same sunny skies and light breezes we'd had before.

Needless to say, my guests declared their heartfelt gratitude; they also declared their willingness to follow my hunches from then on without complaint. They knew that we'd have been in considerable difficulty had we stayed on that exposed north shore.

It remains a strange event to me. I do not know, to this day, what signs I was reading, what patterns I was feeling. I suspect that the uneasiness I felt had something to do with barometric changes, but there was not, in my own mind, any question of having guessed. I *knew* that there was danger approaching, and felt it so strongly that I was ready to risk the displeasure of my guests.

I mention this event for several reasons. First, if I could predict a severe, though very localized, change in weather with my amateur's skills, then the skilled hunter-gatherer would be able to read much more subtle changes, probably down to things I would not be able to recognize as changes even when they were upon me.

Second, it illustrates something seldom recognized about human survival in the wilds; the essential skill is accurate prediction, and it is a *mental* skill, not a physical one. As I noted earlier, the hunter-gatherer's "shopping" was a unique enterprise. Nature provided for virtually all his needs, but nature's materials did not sit on a shelf in peak condition all year long. Whether the item needed was a root, swamp plant, berry, flower, bark, rice, bird or animal, the quality of each varied dramatically from year to year, from season to season and, frequently, from week to week. Survival required harvesting only when the quality of each item was at its highest. Taking things too soon or too late caused problems. Nothing could be rushed; instead, everything had to be accurately anticipated and prepared for.

Nor was it simply a matter of saying, "This berry is ripe." Rather, one had to know when to say, "This berry is *as ripe as it's going to get this year*," and to then take advantage of that short-lived opportunity. Not merely recognition, but accurate prediction, the ability to read all the signs to discern the best time for acting, was everyone's central preoccupation. To be sure, physical skills had to be present as well, whether in fire-building, butchering, skinning, tanning, tracking or whatever, but they were useless until the predictive skill had first put people in a position to get full value for the exercise of those skills.

The hunting enterprise most clearly demonstrates the necessity of those predictive skills. Those who do not hunt tend to think of it as going *after* something. While that is indeed part of the process, it is actually of secondary importance. The more important task involves predicting what your quarry will do so that you can put yourself in a position where, waiting with your gun or bow, you can *receive* it. It is predominantly a task of accommodating yourself to an intensely dynamic and fluid reality, reading the signs, trying to anticipate the most appropriate place to be at the most critical moment. It is a matter of asking, "What will this animal do, on this trail, with this wind, at this time of the day and year, in this kind of slough, coming up to that hill and tree-line, with its particular skill and experience at avoiding danger, if I were to do A, B, or C?" At every step, the task is to collect all observations, read all patterns, sift through all experiences and rank all possibilities in order of likelihood. In short, it is a task of mental anticipation.

Even the apparently simple matter of moving from one place to another through the wilderness required the same mental preparation. The terrain ahead had to be mentally paddled over, walked through, climbed up, slid down and crawled over in the conditions that one anticipated would prevail before the decision to travel was made. It was not a world where one could count on rescue in the event of a miscalculation; it was a world which demanded unceasing caution and forethought. Whenever something significant occurred in the course of the journey which had not been anticipated and planned for, the group would pause and repeat the exercise with the new variable included. The need for assimilation of detail to assist future prediction remained constant and critical.

As I suggested at the beginning of this chapter, it may be that the predominance of this pattern-thought in the enterprise of necessary prediction was itself a cause of the ethics and rules discussed thus far.

Quite clearly, the modelling approach to education seems a natural outgrowth of this approach to survival. The ability to make accurate predictions rests on the accumulation of individual memory, observation and pattern-thought skills. It does not seem to permit teaching, at least as we know it, just as my fellow guides could not teach me what I needed to know to be efficient in my selection of spots. Instead, it requires that one watch, and watch again, as the only way to build up a store of memory-images, to develop perception skills and a capacity for thinking in terms of pattern correspondence. What had to be learned could not be expressed easily, if at all, in words; each person had to immerse himself in the enterprise and develop his own skills.

It is true that some things like skinning a beaver or smoke-curing trout could be verbally taught. If, however, the more critical skill of prediction could not be, I suspect that there was a conscious move away from verbal instruction in all enterprises. Would it not be better training if children learned everything by paying attention on their own? Would it not be wise to have all learning accomplished through the development of those individual observational skills which were essential to the predictive task? Given the complexity of prediction skills, would it not be appropriate to begin their training by having children teach themselves the relatively simpler things as well? If you could not learn to build a fire or skin a beaver just by watching, how could you ever hope to learn how to predict bird or animal behaviour, weather changes, plant maturation, and subtler moments?

We may now be able to appreciate why the absence of verbal instruction was seen as a distinct social good in traditional times,

✦

and to better understand the difficulties Native people have when faced with a society which has developed the opposite view.

The prevalence of pattern-thought may also make it easier to understand other things as well. Just as my fellow guides could not explain why they chose to fish some spots over others, and I could not explain how I knew a storm was approaching, it is my guess that a great many things in the hunter-gatherer way of life might have similarly defied what we call "reasoned" explanation. I postulate, in fact, that the question "Why did you do that?" was rarely asked, simply because the only answer would be something close to "It felt right" or, in perhaps the ultimate expression of how the reasoner perceives his conclusions to be formed, by saying "It came to me."

Whenever someone did ask for advice or counsel, I expect that it was provided in the same fashion I encounter it today, that is, in the form of a story or a description of events which contains no attempt whatever to explicitly state a recommendation. These parable-like recitations provide only the raw materials from which conclusions can be drawn. In traditional times it was necessary that everyone learn to use such raw materials, to draw their own conclusions using their own thoughts. Information could of course be shared, but the method of managing it could not. The need to develop one's own skills in information-processing may well have permeated every aspect of life.

Furthermore, this kind of reasoning does not, I suggest, provide either "right" answers or "wrong" answers in our sense of the words. Instead, they are only more or less productive. Errors in prediction were merely an indication that certain mental or observational skills needed to be further developed. As intimated above, in this pattern-thought kind of reasoning the conclusions which come are precisely that: conclusions which seem to come, on their own and effortlessly. The reasoner himself seems to perceive it this way. When it is impossible as well for the reasoner to set out his train of thought step by step (the very arena in which a critic can say "Ah-hah, that's where you went wrong!"), what scope can there ever be for criticism? Do we criticize people for what they *receive*? If a person chooses to act on the basis of what everyone perceives as "guidance received", how can that person be open to criticism? Was he not simply doing his best to follow the guidance that was granted him? As long as each person did the best he or she could to observe carefully, to recall thoroughly, and to await patiently the apparent guidance which this reasoning process appears to provide, how could criticism be appropriate? People did not make mistakes; they simply had more to learn, greater skills to work on. It was, in fact, a self-rewarding and self-punishing enterprise which everyone had every reason to become better at, day after day and year after year. The survival of all depended upon it.

Seen from this perspective, the reverence with which older people are viewed takes on new force. They were revered not only for what they had done in the past but for what they could still do in the present. Even when their powers of observation began to fail, they possessed two things younger people lacked: a reservoir of experience (or, in the predictive enterprise, of memory-images), and sophisticated skills in pattern-thought which others were only developing. Because of those skills and attributes, older people remained of inestimable value long after their physical powers had deteriorated. Their stories of days gone by were not just wistful reminiscenses; they were mines of information which would, without question, be of value at some time in the future. After all, the world which their children and grandchildren would inherit would be precisely the same world they had survived. No technological revolutions would make their skills redundant and no massive construction projects would change the face of the landscape to make their memories of it irrelevant. What they had seen—and survived—in the past could well come again, and only they had the storehouse of knowledge to help the group anticipate and prepare. As long as their minds remained sharp, the older people became, with each passing day, even more valuable to the practical survival concerns of the group. It is little wonder that they were held in such high esteem.

It is also my suspicion that the very pronounced emphasis that Native people place upon the notion of seeking and receiving guidance, upon possessing "gifts" of prediction, flow from this kind of thought process. As I have said, a person's conclusions are not perceived, even by that person, as products of his own making.

✦

Instead, it is understood that they are somehow visited upon him. The sense of being an architect of one's conclusions is replaced by a sense of having merely made oneself open to receive them. The reasoner himself adopts this attitude of grateful acceptance rather than proud accomplishment. The wise man claims no credit for his wisdom, seeing himself as having been visited by gifts of wisdom that originated beyond him. In that sense, the very pronounced humility of traditional Native people may in actual fact represent not self-deprecation but a simple statement of personal belief.

The logical next question asks what was understood to have been the source of such wisdom, and again the inquiry must focus upon the impact of pattern-thought on people's perception of the universe. I earlier spoke of "imaging" as opposed to imagining. I suggested that the skilled imager visited times and places in advance of going there, and that during such visits he would experience all the sounds, smells, feels, tastes and sights of those times and places *in his mind*. As he crouched on the trail reading a fresh physical sign, he would also be up ahead with his quarry, reading the signs available to it, sensing fully what it sensed. He would, in fact, be able to inhabit two worlds, and for a significant portion of each day he would trek back and forth between them. On the mental plane the wind would blow just as cold, the granite cliffs would be just as high and confining, the swamp smells just as dense and disguising. The moose would mate and the berries would ripen, all in the same patterns as in the physical world, all with the same richness of life.

In other words, for the skilled hunter-gatherer, there was life on two planes, equally vibrant, equally full and, to a large degree, equally accessible. He knew that this was so because he regularly experienced himself occupying both.

We also have to ask *how* the hunter-gatherer experienced—and thus understood—his worlds. Though he lived on a mental as well as a physical plane, I suggest that those planes were "felt" as opposed to abstractly learned. Further, a people whose knowledge is "felt" knowledge, sensory knowledge, will look at the world very differently from those whose knowledge is primarily intellectual; this difference may be central to the Native concept of a spiritual plane.

◆

In this context, I think back to the day when I "felt" something that warned me of the approaching storm. I remember my very strong sensation of "disturbance building". We can suppose that what I was feeling was a change in barometric pressure, but the fact remains that I *felt* the change. The concept of "barometric pressure falling" was not a simply a concept or an idea but a felt something which passed over me, visited me, and "told" me things. Even the word "thing" is poor because it conveys a sense of something static, something which our minds have frozen in time and attributes—and so is not a living presence.

With our quantifying sciences we have learned to see things, to understand things, as distinct from their constant change, from their *life*. We say "the barometric pressure is X," when in fact we have frozen the life out of it for the purpose of measurement. It sits then as a concept in our minds, separated from its dynamism, from its constant change. And we thus separate ourselves from feeling that life and from being able to know things through life.

When I mentioned being invited to the drum ceremony of my fellow guides calling to the river, I did not try to explain my sense of what was being done, of how the river was perceived by them. We whites have an *idea* of a river, and when we think of praying to a river we have something—one thing—in our mind's eye. If, however, the river is known as a *felt* thing, then in fact it will be known in terms of everything it can make us feel, see, taste, hear and smell. It will be perceived as being made up of all those things which can be sensed about it, all of which will show remarkable change from day to day, season to season, and year to year. People who canoe understand that each river is in fact a multitude of rivers; even the same short stretch is subject to surprising change. The sensed aspects of the river which combine and re-combine to show a constantly changing face are perceived not as characteristics of *a* river, but as spirits *within and of* the river. Some would be more predominant (powerful) than others, and lesser ones might appear and disappear in an instant, but all of them are always there, always active, always *alive*. They can be perceived through human senses, no matter how fleeting their appearance, and it is understood that they will always show themselves again at some future time. This is how I understand

✦

what is meant when Native people speak of the spirits of the
river.

Nor is it just "things" which, because they can be sensorily
known, have spirit within them. People can also feel (or taste or
hear, etc.) the *properties* of things. Those properties are things-in-
themseslves, felt things, alive things. They are the powers which
reside within things, possessing a life of their own, powers which
the wise and skilled can call upon or, if seen as threatening, do
battle with.

The air illustrates how I understand this way of perceiving the
world. It can be felt in a multitude of ways. People who spend most
of their lives indoors are aware of only a few of the most obvious
ways: cold drafts, warm breezes, suffocatingly humid heat or bitter
winter blasts. People who spend a lot of time outdoors (especially
those who, like farmers and fishermen, must pay attention to
changes in the air for their livelihood) know many other different
"kinds" of air, and know what to associate them with, what to
expect next. Each of those kinds of air becomes familiar, experienced and known. They bring messages. They "speak". When you
know things because you have *felt* them, you know them as alive,
as having their own life, their own spirit. It is not that cute (or dangerous) little spirits live in them like cartoon characters; it is that
they *have* spirit and, fundamentally, *are* spirits.

At the same time, all like things in nature possesses the
unique spirit of their kind or their species. They are more than
individual things which are simply alike in most ways; they
instead represent all others of their species by virtue of sharing
the spirit which gives life to all of them. So it is when the first
eagle returns in the spring, traditional Native people do not say
"*An eagle* has returned." Nor do they say "*The eagles* have
returned." Instead, they say "*Eagle* has returned," for each eagle
exists because it is powered by Eagle's spirit. Each eagle (and
moose and bear and duck) must be treated with the utmost
respect, simply because it is more than its individual self.

I know that I have not done justice to this aspect of Native
spirituality. I am not certain that contemporary English could
express it properly even if I did understand it. I would like, therefore, to pass along the words of the Ojibway scholar and author,

✦

Mr. Basil Johnston. He wrote to me about Native spirituality, about the real scope and depth of meaning of the Ojibway word "manitou":

> Depending on context, "manitou" may mean, in addition to spirit, supernatural, divine, animating principle, essence, property, attribute, magical, mystical, deity, quiddity, meta-physical, inexplicable, a mystery, etc. If the term "manitou" is not properly understood and used as it ought to be, that is, if it is used in only one sense, that of spirit, it distorts the language as well as the perception and intent of the speaker.

It was, incidentally, Mr. Johnston who asked that I be careful not to "perpetuate the notion that Indians believe little spirits live in trees, rocks, waterfalls and elsewhere". I hope I have captured some small portion of what he, and many others, have been trying to explain to me.

To return to the conviction that there were two planes of existence, each interactive with the other: it seems clear that such a conviction could not help but lead, ultimately, to certain other kinds of conclusions.

If, for instance, it is possible for a man to "walk" through the spiritual (that is, the imaged) plane, then he could not deny the possibility that others would be able to do the same. The dimension of each person which did this visiting thus ought to be able to encounter the corresponding dimension of others; suddenly the possibility of *interaction* with others on that plane becomes real. Further, there would be no reason to conclude that such interaction could only be of a positive sort; it would therefore seem prudent to adopt a stance of vigilance even in thought, lest offence be given on that other plane. Ridding yourself of all negative thoughts would be considered essential, if only to avoid antagonizing the spiritual dimension of others. Because people were vulnerable on two planes, extreme circumspection was a central requirement.

Many other kinds of conclusions and practices appear logical once there is belief in an interactive spiritual plane. Reverence for (and perhaps fear of) ancestors becomes reasonable, for death on

✦

the physical plane does not mean ceasing to exist on the other. Fasting, vision pits and the seeking of protective Naming-Spirits are seen as reasonable precautions. Dreams themselves take on a different significance, being seen not as the products of one's subconscious but as signals that are being channelled through it; why would dreams not be the logical way for inhabitants of the spiritual plane to communicate?

I confess to knowing little about the particular spiritual beliefs traditional to Native people, little about actual spiritual practices, ceremonies and the like. I do know, however, how strong their conviction is in the existence of that interactive spiritual plane. I suspect that no other belief system could have developed given the way in which, as a hunter-gatherer people, they had to think to survive. Basil Johnston also wrote of this other sphere of conviction and involvement:

> The term "manitou" is much broader in meaning and in application than is generally believed, and refers to those realities existing in the world outside human experience in the realm of dream, vision, the after-life, the supernatural.

Euro-Canadian people, for the most part, do not think in such ways. In fact, we probably began to think differently as agriculture developed and so lessened our need to focus on predictive skills. No longer needing to continually adapt ourselves to whatever circumstances were thrown at us by the natural order, we began instead to focus upon skills of manipulation and mastery. As we became less dependent upon accurately reading natural variables, we became less involved in pattern-reasoning. Insulating ourselves increasingly from the natural world, we stopped knowing it by feeling it, and it stopped having the same vibrancy for us. Having no compelling practical need to visit a spiritual plane of existence, it gradually ceased to exist as a prominent factor in daily life.

Similarly, because we began to think differently, we learned to think of ourselves differently. Over time our lives became, at least for many of us, lives lived almost exclusively on the physical plane as far as our notions of self were concerned. At the same time, we began to create a very different mental plane, the plane of *ideas* of things which, because they were never learned through feeling, lacked life and force and spirit. We began to see our choices as precisely that—our choices—and we began to insist that people take ever greater responsibility for them. Those choices thus became open to criticism and we bore the burden of explaining them. Learning to explain them enabled us to begin teaching them, and we did. The question "Why did you do that?" became a sensible and central one; answers such as "Because it felt right" or "Because that was the guidance I received" became unintelligible to us, often the subject of derision. A gulf began to separate the two sorts of reasoners, the two sorts of perceivers. Neither could see it, for each believed that the other thought the way he did, the way he assumed all people do.

I think that we have not fully considered the possibility that the hunter-gatherer context not only required formidable mental activity but a mental activity which differed significantly from the one which grew to predominate after agriculture developed. Nor have we considered that the daily exercise of those unique mental skills would necessarily lead to very different—but equally sophisticated and complex—perceptions of self, of the order of the universe and one's position within it, and of rules governing appropriate behaviour between people. Instead, seeing only primitive shelters and tools, we concluded that there was very little in the way of sophisticated mental activity among Native people. The image of the unreflective savage became accepted, their ability to survive under harsh conditions ascribed instead to some form of animal intuition.

I don't doubt that Native people, in turn, deprecated our explorers and settlers, wondering how they could possess so many powerful tools but still be so dense as to continually be caught unprepared for the coming weeks and seasons. How, they must have repeatedly asked, could we have missed so many clues staring us straight in the face? The predominant reaction of both groups, when regarding the other, must have been one of total bewilderment.

✦

In Part Two I will consider what may be the impact of retaining traditional rules of conduct and ways of thinking in a world which now puts markedly different demands upon Native people. First, however, I want to try to tie the foregoing material into a more comprehensive whole—and to place it within the emotional context that I regularly experience in the North. It is rare to find a Native speaker whose words do not contain at least an implicit lament for the loss of traditional times. Indeed, many families in the North treat the annual late-fall/early-winter trek to the trapline as the highlight of the year. How do all of the things discussed thus far add up to a way of life so valued, so prized? What are the things which our life does not provide? Just as importantly, could *we* be missing something? Given the obvious hardships of traditional life in the bush, its positive aspects, whatever they were, must have been powerful indeed.

CHAPTER 7

POOR, NASTY, BRUTISH AND SHORT?

No arts; no letters; no society; and which is worst of all, continual fear and danger of violent death; and the life of man solitary, poor, nasty, brutish and short.

Thomas Hobbes (1588–1679), *The Leviathan*

To convey how I imagine life must have been in traditional times, I must start with something that struck me only recently, though with surprising force. My wife, three young children and I went on a three-day hike into Pukaskwa National Park on the north shore of Lake Superior. We followed a trail which had been used for more than a hundred years, winding across open rock faces, through dense and silent cedar forests, around the edges of swamps and up and down small canyons. As we walked along, I suddenly felt a strange and seemingly contradictory mixture of fear and elation. It came from imagining something I had never let take hold of me before, despite having hiked, hunted, and canoed in many parts of northwestern Ontario, some of which were unquestionably more remote.

I imagined that the path, my family and I were all there really was. I imagined that at the end of the day there would be no schools, no warm, dry houses, no hospitals, no pensions, no clothing stores, no supermarkets. At the end of the trail there would be no road, no Kenora, no Toronto, no New York, no Tokyo. There would only be more of what I could see around me, stretching off into some boundless infinity of both time and place. There might

✦

be other tiny groups of people here and there, other extended families, but they would have no more than I did. My family and I were essentially on our own, forever.

I had often thought about physical survival in the bush, imagining myself temporarily stranded for one or two weeks until someone found me. Anyone who travels regularly in the North has done the same. I had never, however, really considered what it would feel like if that were a *permanent* state. Behind my earlier thoughts of survival I had always taken for granted the presence of the outside world, of the potential it provided both for rescue and for a simple change of scene. Suddenly imagining a world in which the "outside" simply did not exist was a shock. In a world where there was nothing but wilderness, there would be nowhere else to go, no other context in which to seek fulfilment. Further, the enterprises of life would not change from generation to generation. Each life would end in a world unchanged from my ancestors' time. My great-great-grandchildren, and theirs in turn, would inhabit exactly the same world and would need the same skills, fight the same struggles, and live lives essentially identical to mine. They would not have a better life than I did, nor would they even have a different one. They would do and be what I had done and been, in the same places, in the same ways forever, just as it had always been.

This is not the way we think of our lives today, or of life in general. We see ourselves on a road, moving forward, progressing down some linear track that promises constant improvement and discovery, from cancer cures to life on Mars. Our eyes are forward, the past is of largely academic interest, the present only an instant we race through to arrive at a different tomorrow. In our belief system we dedicate ourselves to a single task: creating change.

But what if we did not have that conviction underlying our every thought, the conviction that tomorrow, for each of us, if we all work hard, there will be more and better everything? What if our conviction was not that we were born to continue travelling down an infinitely changing road, but instead, that our destiny was to repeat what had been done before, to walk in the footsteps of all who had gone before, to think the same thoughts they had

✦

already thought; to take, in effect, their place on the slowly revolving wheel of eternally repeating existence? What if we defined our lives not as occupying the new ground of our own discoveries but as revisiting ground already occupied by all our ancestors? Our predominant sense of self would be largely shaped by the conviction that we were going where others had gone before and where others would always go. We would be taking our turn at the wheel of life rather than moving ahead from where others had left off. The shape of existence would be circular, not *evolving*, but *revolving*. The past, present and future would always be essentially the same. Just as the four seasons come, go and always return again, so too each generation would come and go, never striking out on its own path. Instead, it would retrace the path of the last. Each generations's turn at the wheel might include performances better or worse than those of the last, but they would be essentially the same performances, with the same set and script and plotting.

To use another analogy, it would be something like a relay race which never ends, each generation passing the baton to the next for its turn around the track, the old and new generations running side by side while the transfer takes place, the older one slowing as the newer picks up speed. Each would go where the other had already gone, would come to see and hear and think what had already been seen and heard and thought by countless earlier generations. No matter who travelled it or when, the track would be common to all. It is little wonder, then, that the "track" would become sacred, for it would have been shared by all and have given sustenance to all since time beyond memory, just as it must provide sustenance into the infinite future. This is more than just an emotional tie to the land; the land itself is a tie to the communal past, present and future.

We post-industrial societies, in contrast, seem to run a cross-country relay race, passing the baton to a generation that will never set foot upon the ground we have covered, a generation that will not know where we have been, that will never see our footprints. As we pass them the baton and watch them speed away, we have no sense of them visiting where we have been or coming, ultimately, to where we now rest. They simply go their own way, leaving us guessing about what they will find and about whether they will be equipped to handle it. The more remote their lives become from what we have known, the less confident we feel that we can know and understand them. And the more we are tempted to feel alone and in some fashion unconnected.

There may be a synergy of sorts here: the more we cover new ground, the more we feel unconnected to either a familiar past or future, then the more we may also feel a pressing need to leave our mark by building or exploring something new. By going further, faster or higher than anyone has gone before, we may merely be wishing to find some way to erect a sign that says "I was here."

But if, by contrast, we did not think that we travelled a new road alone but an old road worn smooth by our ancestors, would we not be less concerned with such testaments to our presence? Would we have the same preoccupation with what is new, with leaving our singular mark for all to see? Or would we instead find our sense of continuity in the fact that our descendants would not have to "look back" to know of us, for they would be walking on our trails. The stories about us would not fade, because their relevance would not diminish. Our lives and the lessons we learned would live on in those stories, a part of our children's lives as they covered the same ground. In a sense, they would relive our lives, as we had relived those of our ancestors, experiencing what we experienced where we experienced it. The only imperative, then, would involve not leaving a monument but instead an undefiled terrain, as suitable for their use as it was for ours.

This, then, is how I imagine that Native people in traditional times viewed their part in the cycle of life. Each person would live where his or her ancestors lived, face what they faced, develop and use the skills they used, following literally in their paths. There is a temptation to conclude that such a repetitive existence would be boring in the extreme, that it would feel binding and imprisoning. We, addicted to novelty, have a hard time imagining how such a life could ever be considered attractive. Man, we think, is by definition a restless soul always in search of new frontiers, new challenges. We suspect we would go mad doing only what our fathers and mothers did, repeating their lives. How, we ask ourselves, can Native people lament the passing of a time when they lived under those limits?

I suspect, however, that they had no such sense of limits. In fact, they may have perceived their lives as holding a virtually limit*less* scope for challenge and accomplishment. We don't see this, if only because we don't share the same definition of accomplishment. As I suggested in the last chapter, their lives did not centre on building things but upon discerning things. Life's challenge lay in observing and understanding the workings of the dynamic equilibrium of which they were a part, then acting so as to sustain a harmony within it rather than a mastery over it. One aspired to wisdom in accommodating oneself to that equilibrium, and that pursuit quite clearly promised unlimited scope for exploration and self-development.

Further, I suspect that they sought that wisdom not only to better insure survival but also as an end in itself, as something in itself exhilarating. I recall how I felt after accurately predicting that violent hail-storm, and it was exactly that: exhilarated. It was not just that I was thankful to have side-stepped its full, destructive force. More significant by far was the excitement I felt at being able to say to myself "I was right! I am learning! I am becoming more open and discerning, more in tune with the workings of this universe around me!" Even that one, small accomplishment was thrilling. I'm not certain why, but I do know that the feeling far surpassed what I have felt in other endeavours, such as getting good grades or delivering a well-received speech. The sense of achievement seemed to come not because I had *done* something, but because I had *become* something. In some way, I felt that I had become more a part of our vibrant universe in that I had grown more attuned to it.

What matters most is not so much why that feeling of exhilaration occurred, but the fact that it did occur. There was, without doubt, a very strong sense of achievement and of personal growth— all within the context of a "no-growth" enterprise. We who focus so much on building, accumulating, erecting monuments, and so on have a hard time seeing that there might be other sources of self-esteem, of pride in achievement. In fact, each hunter-gatherer may have had more opportunities for achieving an expanded sense

✦

of self than most of us will ever know. I have worked in an office in Toronto, and I have worked as a fishing guide. My achievement horizons in Toronto were visible almost from the outset, my days filled with repetitive tasks which, once mastered, held no further interest and posed no further challenge. While it might appear that going out each day to take tourists fishing is similarly repetitive, I did not perceive each day that way. The variables of weather within which I had to operate and the process of pattern-thought which guided me showed both immense variety and an almost limitless scope for challenge and for improvement. Unlike my office experiences, I knew that I would never be able to say that I had mastered the enterprise. There would always be opportunity to observe more closely, to remember more clearly, to further refine the process of pattern-thought. I felt I could always progress, always achieve more, always become in some critical sense "more" than I was the day before.

There is another aspect of life in the wilderness which must be mentioned: it invites (or requires) that your senses be held open at virtually all times. I was not aware that this was a different posture until, after a summer's guiding, I returned to Toronto to visit my old haunts. I walked past the bars and stores and restaurants that had once been my favourite parts of the city, and I began to feel surprisingly uncomfortable. There were more noises, smells, people, colours, and activities than I could absorb with comfort. For the first while I hungrily devoured all of the stimuli I could find. After all, that was one of the reasons for visiting the city. But that level of chaotic stimulation was not sustainable. I was forced to pull back on my summer habit of trying to distinguish and register the full variety of smells penetrating my nostrils and sounds assaulting my ears. Instead of letting my gaze roam, trying to pick up motion and colour and light, I had to concentrate on a narrow path in front of me. It was not just that I was no longer used to such stimuli; instead, I was no longer in the habit of shutting down my senses to control the degree of stimulus they were subjected to. I couldn't wait to get back out of the city, to be able to let my guard down again, to return to a posture of openness, curiosity and welcome. It is a wonderful psychological stance to be able to maintain towards

✦

the events of each day, a stance of open welcome instead of guarded denial, and it leads to a sense of involvement with life rather than intentional (and necessary) distancing from it. The urban environment's constant over-stimulation of the senses cannot help but cause us to *limit* the use of our senses, to intentionally shut ourselves down. In that sense, we adopt a guarded stance towards life rather than an open one, and we become less than we could be.

If we consider traditional life in the bush from these perspectives, it appears not to be a life of limited horizons and the mindless repetition of deadening, menial tasks. Instead, it can be seen as a vibrant world of challenges both physical and mental, full of opportunity for exhilaration and accomplishment, experienced at all times from a psychological stance of openness and a philosophical posture of accommodation and harmony, rather than dominance and disintegration.

I have not even mentioned the spiritual component of the life; it obviously provided still another dimension for challenge and development. That enterprise above all others showed no limits or boundaries.

In short, although Natives' physical lives may well have fallen within Hobbes's vision of life in nature, it is just as likely that their mental, emotional and spiritual lives permitted challenges and rewards that were richer than those most of us know in our late twentieth-century lives. Their "no-growth" physical world, however demanding and technologically impoverished, might well have provided them with an enviable sense of personal challenge and accomplishment.

The story does not end there. Oddly enough, the hunter-gatherer may have had a substantially greater sense of personal and family security than we know now. While I have spoken at length about the predominant concern for simple survival, it was in one critical respect a far less worrisome concern than we know today: each family may have sensed that its survival was something over which it had substantial control. If the family worked hard and well, thinking ahead and preparing with care, it could probably handle whatever came its way. To be sure, there was the possibility of attack by another tribe or a winter of unusual duration and severity, but even those survival concerns admitted the chance for successful response. By contrast, we have a number of survival concerns which we feel powerless to control as individuals, including nuclear holocaust, the escape of an uncontrollable virus and the discovery that we are too late to reverse catastrophic environmental degradation.

While the circular vision of existence leads to the conviction that there will be no new challenges in the future which have not been met successfully in the past, the linear view destroys that conviction. Believing that the future will always contain new developments, we are forced to face the possibility that we will be unable to cope with some of them. When new developments continue to emerge with increasing speed and frequency, that concern can only escalate. I suspect that such concern, and the inevitable stress that accompanies it, was unknown to hunter-gatherer peoples. Despite (or because of) our technological wizardry, we may face the future with far less confidence than they did. The threats which they faced were fewer in number and more amenable to direct control and response. They could plan and act with much greater confidence, seeing themselves as masters of their own fates to a degree which we may never know. After all, the world they inhabited had supported countless generations of their ancestors, and virtually nothing about that world had changed.

The sense of security that came from seeing life as a revolving affair was constantly reinforced by a multitude of things. The seasons followed one another in regular succession. So did every other aspect of the natural world, from ripening berries to spawning fish to mating caribou. Every part of creation repeated itself from year to year, returning in forms, numbers and conditions that were already familiar. In that repetition there was promise and a reason for faith. As each part of each season brought resources to their optimal condition for harvesting, families moved across the landscape in ritual and celebrated re-attendance at familiar locations. It is easy to see why each person would develop an attitude of respect for his or her surroundings; all of those surroundings were, in fact, *home*. At the same time, they were everything else too, from recreation centre to supermarket

✦

to place of worship. The necessity of preserving those surroundings unaltered for the sustenance of future generations made respect the essential commandment, and waste and despoliation the worst sin. For the wheel of life to continue revolving, it was necessary to interfere as little as possible. Each article taken, whether a bird, plant, animal or fish, was taken with regret and with respectful thanks given in obligatory ceremony. Anyone who took more than was necessary put everyone else in peril when the wheel turned and the family came to that place again.

This imperative of respect for nature, or non-interference in that realm too, stands in direct contrast to our habit of seeking change for its own sake. We have, for centuries, operated under the illusion that we could leave our mistakes behind us, that the harmful by-products of our activities would never come back to haunt us. Following our linear illusion, we assumed that we could do as we wished, then move on to someplace new and unspoiled. It may be that the lessons we are belatedly learning about greenhouse gases, deforestation and ozone depletion are now challenging that linear view. Even our economists are now beginning to talk in terms of sustainable growth. In the end, we may be required to adopt the traditional Native notion of the revolving wheel of life and, with it, their insistence upon walking softly across the landscape.

The degree to which formal celebrations of thanksgiving were a central and frequent fact of traditional life are evidence of the grateful attitude. Feast days occurred at regular intervals, celebrating a wide variety of events, from the return of certain birds marking the arrival of spring to the winter solstice marking the passing of the shortest day. Such regular observances unquestionably lent life a celebratory and festive air which few of us associate with survival living. Imagine, for example, the feast celebrating the first taste of fresh fish in the spring, or the successful end of the fall caribou hunt. Imagine returning to the familiar berry patch or paddling around a bend in the river to see the wild rice ready for harvest once again. Imagine, too, the celebration when the harvest was complete and the family's survival for another season was assured as a result of the family's team effort, everyone contributing, side by side.

✦

In contrast, I have the sense that in this alienated and over-technological society people feel they have precious few occasions for celebration, and fewer still that involve *shared* celebration with their families for family-based achievements. Our accomplishments seem so often to be individual ones, whether in business or school or sports. But we still need celebration, to join with others in team enterprises. In fact, we have created Stanley Cups, Super Bowls and a host of other competitions in an attempt to satisfy that need. It does not seem unreasonable to ask, however, whether the vicarious thrill of seeing Wayne Gretzky score a series-winning goal in overtime is comparable to participating in your own family's successful caribou hunt and the stockpiling of enough skins and meat to approach the coming winter with confidence. In that respect, we might well ask which group knows the richer experience of shared triumph and celebration.

These, then, are the kinds of things, good and positive things, which most of us fail to see when we try to imagine a physically precarious life in the survival context. They are the kinds of things, however, which still make the eyes of the old people sparkle when they remember, and cloud over when they think of their grandchildren taking on our ways and abandoning theirs. They are the kinds of things that make them shake their heads in quiet bewilderment when they see us despoil and pollute this planet in the name of what we call progress.

I did not mean to conclude that their lives were rich in every respect, and ours poor, or that all of their approaches were wise and all of ours folly. Nor do I mean to romanticize their brutal, frequently tragic, lives. My intention instead is to underline that their laments are both real and valid, as are their concerns for what the future holds. In one sense, their criticism of our careless and polluting ways is an easy one for them to make, given that they lacked the technology to interfere as massively as we have done. It will never be known whether they too would have fallen into our destructive ways if they had enjoyed the same opportunities for material progress. It remains true, however, that their traditional attitudes and conclusions, however formed, deserve much closer attention.

✦

But the times of old appear to have gone for good. Even though many Native people genuinely and legitimately lament their passing, those days will not return. I have seen no back-to-the-trapline movement, no yearning to return to the nomadic, survival existence of days gone by. The kids want out, and most parents want them to be able to go out. The question now becomes, if the physical lifestyle of traditional times is to be permanently abandoned, what *other* portions of that life can be productively carried forward?

There are a number of common assumptions about what happens when two radically different cultures collide. One suggests that the minority culture is inevitably assimilated by the majority one. I hope to have shown that there are many aspects of Native culture which not only can survive but that also should, in my view, be adopted by the majority. These include respect for the natural sphere, an emphasis upon careful and sensitive consensus-building, a focus upon a rehabilitative and preventative response to social turmoil and an insistence upon family and community responsibility for the mental, emotional, spiritual and physical health of each member.

Another assumption is that the minority culture has the opposite choice, that of building walls around itself and remaining untouched, unaltered and whole, as some Mennonite and Hasidic communities have chosen to do so. This does not appear to be the choice of most Native people, however, for they seem eager to leave behind the constant battle for survival and to enjoy such benefits of our society as its extensive educational opportunities. It seems clear that some mixing of the two is both inevitable and probably welcome. The question, once again, involves deciding what must be adopted from the outside culture, what must be adapted to, what must be retained in its original purity from traditional times and what must be returned to that state.

It is at this point that a third assumption presents itself, namely, that it is the sudden stripping away of traditional culture which is *exclusively* responsible for the social chaos that exists on far too many northern reserves. This assumption holds that since such chaos did not exist in traditional times, it can only be

✦

the erosion of that culture that is the source of the problem. In Part Two of this book, I explore the possibility that a portion of the social chaos apparent today may be the direct result of *retaining* some traditional rules after people started living in a very different physical context. Traditional codes of behaviour were developed in a setting which bears little resemblance to the reality of today's Native communities. No doubt a great many traditional beliefs and approaches, had they not been intentionally attacked and destroyed, could have helped substantially in the transition period. At the same time, however, it is my present view that there are other beliefs which have been maintained past their usefulness to the point that they are now dramatically counter-productive.

As always, nothing is ever as clear or as one-sided as it seems. Coming to an accurate understanding of the social forces at work in today's northern Native communities may be well nigh impossible, especially for a WASP outsider like me. But, to repeat my old refrain, I would rather be wrong, and corrected, than simply wrong in silence. At one community in my district, 129 people stood charged with 222 offenses under the Criminal Code of Canada one cold January day in 1986. That figure represented one out of every ten people living there. If ten percent of the population of Ottawa or Toronto had to go to criminal court on any one day, the nation would declare itself in a state of social emergency. Without doubt, there would be a frenzy of discussion about how such a state had come to pass and what could be done to turn things around. The northern reserves are no less deserving of our efforts and our concern. Getting an accurate understanding of the sources of that turmoil is one of our most pressing duties.

PART TWO

UNDERSTANDING THE PRESENT

■

CHAPTER 8

THE CHANGED PHYSICAL CONTEXT

In September 1982 I had an opportunity to appear as Crown Attorney at four settlements along the James Bay coast. Each night I returned to the Oblate Fathers' mission at Fort Albany, where I met Father Lavoie, already in his eighties. He had served the Native communities on that coast for over fifty years, and spoke fluent Cree. One evening after dinner he took me to his tiny study and produced a photograph album spanning those fifty years. I was particularly struck by two old photographs.

The first was a winter scene in the bush which he had entitled "Visiting My Parishioners". It showed an Indian woman and her infant peering happily through the flap of a caribou-skin tent at the snowy world outside. He explained that it was taken on their trapline, some two hundred miles inland from the coast.

From that photo an important fact became clear to me: until relatively recently, northern Indians did not live in the year-round, multi-family communities we see today. Instead, each person spent the major portion of his life surrounded only by his or her own extended family, deep in the bush, cut off from all other families. It was within that unique context that the rules of conduct discussed so far came into being.

♦

The second photograph that made an impression on me was a summer scene in the location of the present mission. It showed some thirty Indian children under a tarpaulin stretched between some trees, all of the children seated in neat rows on half-log benches behind half-log desks. This was their school. It operated only during the summer months, because it was only during that period that families came in off the traplines for an extended visit to that central location. In the fall, winter and spring months there was no one left to teach, because the families had once again dispersed over the landscape.

Even those summer congregations were not what we might expect. First of all, they were the exception to normal life rather than the rule. Further, they were not always the happy reunions we think of them as being. Inter-family mistrust and, on occasion, overt antagonism, were not uncommon. Although these summer meetings were necessary to provide opportunities for trade, certain cooperative undertakings and the finding of non-family marriage partners, it appears that each family took great care to be certain that it occupied its own separate point of land or stretch of shoreline. What existed over those summer months was not a community as we would define the term, or as we believe exists today across the North.

Traditional ethics, then, were formulated with three different contexts in mind: central ethics governing life within one's own extended family, then ethics governing occasional, controlled interaction with other families perceived to be essentially cooperative and, finally, ethics governing the very rare occasions of contact with outsiders. At no time prior to European contact, or even during the trapping era after contact, was there any need to develop ethics and rules appropriate to ongoing, daily relations with people *other than* those within one's own extended family. That, however, is precisely the context within which most Indian people in the North now find themselves. Their reserve communities regularly have populations as high as twelve hundred people in my region, with the majority in the five hundred range.

It is crucial that we understand that this is a *new* context for them. Further, the present-day, year-round and multi-family communities that constitute today's northern reserves are *our*

✦

creations, not theirs. Most important, we must recognize that these settlements did not evolve slowly; they were created almost overnight.

In many other regions of Canada, Native communities grew into existence on their own, often as agriculture developed. Agriculture meant that a much smaller geographic area could support a larger number of people, for families no longer had to spread out across the landscape to guard against over-hunting. Instead, they could remain in a smaller area for most of the year, relying increasingly on their crops. Larger communities formed over time of their own momentum. During that developmental time new rules governing inter-family behaviour could be slowly developed and adjusted to. People had the luxury of growing into this larger society slowly and with care. The Mohawk, for instance, had been an agricultural people long before the first Europeans arrived, and had developed a very complex system of governance extending to a great many people, including a formal and sophisticated justice system. This was not the case in the North. Families remained, even after adopting the barter life of the trapline, essentially non-agricultural, living in separate extended-family societies, served by the same rules and ethics that had been tested and proven sound for thousands of years. Suddenly, in the 1960's and early 1970s, all that changed.

Until that time, our federal and provincial governments, anxious to assimilate Indian children into our society, operated residential schools at central locations like Kenora. Indian children were brought to those school from all over northern Ontario. They operated for the most part during our regular school year, permitting children to return home for the summer vacation. Coincidentally, their parents and older siblings continued trapping while the younger ones were away at school.

There were problems, however, with both the policy of forced assimilation and with the whole notion of forcing Indian children to spend most of each year divorced from their roots. A decision was made to close those residential schools. So it was that in the late 1960s and 1970s the federal government decided to build day schools at remote locations all across the North, usually wherever the summer campgrounds were in evidence.

✦

The problem was that those "community" day schools did not follow the example of the Oblate Fathers and operate only during the non-trapping portions of the year. Instead, they operated during *our* traditional school year. That school year coincides almost exactly with the trapping season. As that first photograph of Father Lavois illustrated, family traplines were often several hundred miles back in the bush. To operate them properly, trapping families had to live there. As a result, parents faced an excruciating dilemma each time a school opened: give up the trapline or deny their children school (which also happened to be unlawful). There was, for most parents, no way to do both. Forced to choose, most parents opted for school, seeing that as their children's key to the future. Thus, as each school opened across the North, whole groups of families stopped doing what had for generations defined them to themselves: supporting themselves with their traplines and living separate from other families, alone in the bush. Instead, they prepared to settle down, side by side with those other families, year round, for the first time ever.

But there were other changes ahead. Now that there were to be permanent settlements occupied over the cold winter months, it was clear that summertime shelters at those locations would no longer suffice. A major construction undertaking spread across the North as the federal government built hundreds of tiny houses. Those houses, however, were not organized into separate neighbourhoods for traditionally separate families. Instead, they were all built together along streets, in grid patterns reminiscent of city subdivisions. Those streets stretched back from the river, ignoring the river's practical and spiritual importance. Inter-family separation gave way to cheek-by-jowl living, and the scope for friction between different families escalated dramatically. People who had for millenia lived almost exclusively with members of their own family and well away from strangers were now waking up hearing strangers outside their very doorsteps.

It was in this fashion that the federal government created the remote reserve communities we see now across northwestern Ontario. No doubt these efforts aimed at increasing educational opportunities and improving housing were well-intended. Unfortunately, they were made in ignorance of the economic,

✦

psychological, and physical reality of the trapping year and the careful spatial separation which had always been maintained between family groups.

It would not be long before many of the children, in whose interest these communities had been constructed, began coming home from school to find their parents undergoing a grotesque change. Denied access to their traplines, these men and women were robbed of virtually all sources of self-sufficiency, pride and self-esteem. The challenges and rewards of their trapline lives were replaced by endless, empty days, welfare, and a struggle with alcohol that quickly assumed the magnitude of an epidemic. It is nothing short of awful to contemplate how different things might have been if the government had chosen to operate those day-schools during the non-trapping summer period. The trapping season could not have been changed, for pelt quality and travelling conditions are season-dependent. The school year, however, could have been. Children might indeed have had the best of both worlds—our education while staying at home and, for the remainder of the year, the trapping experience of more traditional times. Instead, while the children received our education, their parents, and all they stood for and could have taught them, disintegrated.

It is extremely difficult for city dwellers to appreciate the magnitude of change involved in suddenly becoming part of a year-round, multi-family community. We are used to strangers, to spending substantial portions of our lives not with blood-relatives but out on our own, as individuals, enjoying (and at the same time having to struggle with) our autonomy; we start learning such a life when we first go off to junior kindergarten. This was not, however, the case for people suddenly coming in off the trapline. What awaited them was, sadly and avoidably, a kind of social cliff over which everyone fell at virtually the same instant in each community. The losses experienced and the profound effects these changes had on these communities are the subject of the next chapter.

CHAPTER 9

THE SUDDEN LOSSES

A. INDIVIDUAL FREEDOM OF CHOICE

In a sense there was very little freedom of choice in traditional times, since mere survival required so much effort. Anyone who has spent time camping knows how much of each day must be dedicated to collecting firewood, food preparation, campsite maintenance and so on; it seems that you've no sooner taken care of one meal than it's time to start working on the next. It is possible to get the sense that we will never really have a moment's rest. When we think of adding to that list of chores the acquisition of all our food and clothing directly from the natural world, we feel overwhelmed. We feel that we would be virtual slaves to our basic needs.

The odd fact, however, is that those who enjoy trekking through the wilderness experience not so much a sense of enslavement as of release. I suspect that what we feel we have shed is the experience of being ordered about, of being constantly told what to do, by other persons. We may indeed have done nothing more than trade one set of constraints for another, but we experience taking on the task of basic survival as a gaining of freedom, freedom from the interference, advice and commands of other people.

✦

Even though basic survival puts extreme demands upon us, they are demands to which we can at least choose our own responses. This is different from our daily lives in the post-industrial world, where at every step we are told by others what we must do. When we are on our own in the bush, we feel free to chose, as individuals, how we will respond to the demands of nature and our basic needs.

When Indian people came in off the trapline and took up residence in the new communities, they lost this kind of freedom. Almost overnight their scope for free choice was substantially curtailed. They began to live to a startling degree at the mercy of the choices of others. Virtually all jobs are administered by Chief and council; it is they who decide who gets those jobs. If you do manage to get one, other people decide when you come to work, what you do and how you do it. Similarly, band councils are responsible for housing; they decide who gets a house, what it looks like and where it is situated in the community. Children are told where to go to school and when, and others decide both what those children will be taught and how. As time passed, life became more and more controlled by the choices of others. Community bylaws were enacted. Police came, and then the courts and lawyers and probation officers. Snow machines replaced dogsleds and snowshoes; fuelling and repairing them rested on the choices of others. Government agencies decided if and when each community got more schoolrooms, better health care or more serviceable roads. Deprived of their traditional economic base, communities became almost totally dependent on government largesse for their survival.

This change is even more fundamental than it might first appear. When we speak of being dependent we think primarily in terms of economic dependency. The dependency suffered by northern Indians, however, encompasses much more than government transfer payments. It includes a multitude of things we have grown so accustomed to that we no longer see them as limiting or confining. Stop signs, sidewalks and traffic signals, for instance, are seen by us not as limits on our freedom but as contributing to public safety and efficient movement. For that reason we look on in amazement as a northern band takes two years to debate

✦

whether or not it will erect a stop sign at an intersection where there have already been collisions. I suspect that what we are seeing is a signal of a very basic struggle, the struggle over the propriety of deciding to do to each other what they feel has been one of the most impoverishing things we have done to them: the taking away of individual free choice. It is one thing to have to act within nature's constraints. It is another thing to live under constraints imposed by the outsiders who supply the money. It may be quite another thing still to impose constraints on the freedom of your own people. It must be almost like betraying yourself.

This dynamic may pose one of the major complications for Native people pressing their claim for self-government. Although we hear this call regularly, at the same time we see most bands refusing to exercise or even explore the powers that they already possess under the Indian Act to pass community bylaws. By and large, the only bylaws regularly enacted across the North are for the banning of alcohol on reserve land. There seems to be a sentiment that it is not proper to make laws, to restrict the freedom of others, except in cases where the threat is so great that the very future of the community is at stake.

By way of example, a number of band councils have asked that we do something about parents who, while they are on a drinking spree, leave their young children unattended. In each of these cases, I have explained that charges under the Criminal Code of Canada, the federal statute dealing with criminal behaviour, require a likelihood that the neglect will lead to death or permanent injury; the result is that there would be no chance of successfully prosecuting most such cases of temporary abandonment. When I explain that there is *provincial* law covering exactly the situations that concern them, most bands insist that they do not want provincial laws applied on their reserves, because they see themselves as subject only to federal jurisdiction. I then suggest that they pass their *own* bylaws under those sections of the Indian Act which give bands jurisdiction over such matters as health, public safety and the like. Those charges would then be heard in the community by a Native Justice of the Peace who could levy fines up to $1,000.00 or jail terms up to six months, or combinations of the two. I have even gone so far as to draft a sample bylaw for band consideration. To date, not one band has attempted to enact such a bylaw. Their council members remain adamant that something be done about the problem, but they refuse to respond by enacting their own self-regulating laws.

Those of us from the outside world are perplexed. What we may be missing is their reluctance to contribute to the sudden, almost overwhelming, deprivation of individual free choice which has befallen them since the new communities were built. As I suggested earlier, the push for self-government may at times reflect more of a desire to be left alone than to substitute Native laws and authority figures for non-Native ones.

There may be another reason for this reluctance to enact community bylaws. In an effort to make our courts more responsive to community notions of propriety, Judge Donald Fraser of the Ontario Court (Provincial Division) and I started some experiments on a number of reserves. Our courts may be held in a gymnasium, a band hall, a church, a school library or a nursing station, but our furniture always consists of long trestle tables with folding legs. We began to set them up so that they formed a large square, which is as close to a circle as we can get. We then invited Elders or council members to sit with the court, occupying positions kitty-corner to the judge, with a translator in between. They now advise the court on all sentencings. They are free to speak with the offender, the victim or anyone they choose. While the offender always faces the judge, we make certain that the Crown Attorney and the defense lawyers are not stationed opposite each other; all "geographical" statements of adversariness are removed. Every word spoken is translated, so that anyone can come, listen, understand and contribute. No one need stand when they wish to speak, for we all remain seated and speak to each other as equal partners in a search for protective community responses. We are flexible about when people may speak, and the lawyers are encouraged not to speak in terms of "submissions to the judge" but in terms of "suggestions to the court", which court includes *all* participants. In a similar vein, when people are placed on probation and required to do certain things like seeking counselling or performing free work for the community, we structure it not as an "order of the court" but as the offender's promise to his Elders.

After conducting such a court several times in one community, I had a discussion with their young Chief about self-government and the potentially wide powers his band might wish to explore under the Indian Act. His response went something like this: "Now that I can see we are having more of a community court, perhaps we will consider this." This comment suggested that another factor at work in the refusal of bands to exercise the law-making powers they already possess was that they were reluctant to see their laws administered by strangers from the outside. Time alone will tell whether the development of procedures more in line with their ways of thinking will assist them in implementing self-governing bylaws.

It remains a fact, however, that northern bands are not yet passing their own laws except in cases of the most dire necessity, such as widespread alcohol abuse. Law-making to promote community well-being, as opposed to law-making to stave off an extreme danger, is still, apparently, a foreign notion. Perhaps it is seen as an evil in itself because of its impact on the preponderant characteristic of traditional times, individual free choice.

B. An Internal Esteem System

When the first white fur trader paddled his canoe up to an Indian encampment on a river bank in search of furs, he sought out and began to bargain with the person who could communicate with him the best. It did not matter to the trader if that person was the best trapper, the best provider, the wisest or the most moral person in the camp. It only mattered that he was capable of advancing the trapper's interests. Here we find another of the most disruptive dynamics of contact: the emergence of the need for "specialists" in dealing with the outsiders.

Although in traditional society there were clear roles assigned between the genders, and recognition of people possessing special skills in enterprises like flint-chipping, arrow-making, drumming and other activities, the number of necessary skills was small enough that everyone was expected to achieve some proficiency

✦

in most of them. Family survival demanded it. As a result, the person who was esteemed most highly was the one whose proficiency in *all* things, including things spiritual and moral, was the most pronounced. In contrast to our post-industrial world, it was a world where the generalist was king.

When the first fur trader arrived, that world began to unravel. Suddenly, a new skill emerged as essential to survival of the group: the skill of dealing successfully with the outside world. Just as suddenly, a new source of power emerged, for he who could bargain best with people from the outside brought the greatest wealth to his group. This process culminated in the Indian Act, which required that each band elect a Chief and council to act as its official representative in dealing with our governments. This political process supplanted the traditional conferring of status upon those whose wisdom and moral authority were most pronounced. Suddenly, the development of essentially political and bureaucratic skills became more essential than dealing wisely and productively with the natural world. Whoever developed those new skills also developed power over his own people. They, in turn, became increasingly dependent upon his successful use of those skills. Traditional authority lines were challenged (at our insistence) by those other people who, wise or not, revered or not, *moral* or not, showed the greatest aptitude for dealing successfully with the outside.

A society constructed on the premise that each person ought to work towards self-reliance in virtually all things was confronted by another organizational structure, one based on specialization, on the premise that group progress requires each individual to focus his attention upon learning more and more about less and less. It was the path of the expert, and of dependency, a path upon which "going it alone" was seen as an act of folly rather than independent strength. It was a world in which ever-narrowing skills supplanted general proficiency and wisdom as a source of esteem.

I don't think we fully appreciate the confusion, the sense of lost direction and of social unravelling, that resulted when people of one scheme of social organization came into contact with people of another. In this situation, to whom could they look for

✦

guidance, the traditional wise man or the young kid who has a knack for getting white bureaucrats to open their wallets? Whom does the community need more, the family that can successfully manage a trapline or the collection of separate individuals who can operate word processors, run accounting systems, get houses built on time, supervise school curricula and grab sensational media attention? What do you do with the old people who, although still revered, earned that reverence in enterprises that appear, at least to the young, to bear little relevance to the bureaucratic necessities of the day? In turn, what, if any, reverence is owed to the new heroes, or is reverence itself a thing of the past? To whom, if anyone, are duties of loyalty owed, or do those notions too cease to be pertinent in the new social order? Do you determine your loyalties strictly on the basis of what others can do for you at any particular point in time? Do other people retain an intrinsic worth based on moral goodness, or do they possess only capacities for production?—a view of humans which gives rise to jealous emulation and self-benefiting manipulation. To what *kinds* of ends should each person aspire? What sources exist both for self-esteem and for earning the esteem of others?

It is, in my view, a terrible confusion which many face, for the traditional answers that worked for thousands of years have been challenged with such ferocity that it is amazing that any social cohesion remains at all. The value structures that gave each person a sense of place in his group have all but disintegrated in many communities. Because it occurred so quickly, there has been little opportunity for consensus to form over appropriate replacement schemes. Instead, there is something like a social free-for-all as contrasting views fight for recognition as the appropriate new sources of social cohesion.

At its most basic, an underlying question characterizing many on-reserve struggles seems to be, "Whom should we now respect, revere and seek to emulate...and why?" I hasten to add that my own society seems unable to reach a consensus on those kinds of questions, but we have lived without such a consensus for so long that I doubt we feel any conscious sense of loss. Native communities in the North, however, clearly had that consensus until a short time ago, and they feel the loss deeply.

◆

I should note something else that may prove significant in this respect. There appears to be, in many Native communities today, a concerted effort to restore Elders to the elevated position they formerly held within each community, to recover both for them and for the community itself some of their traditional teachings and practices.

I recall, for example, one man who described the challenge of trying to recover traditional wisdom—and his own health and sanity—in a very moving fashion. When he was a young child living at the south end of Lake of the Woods some fifty years ago, he used to sneak off with other children at night to a hilltop where some of their Elders were known to gather in secret. From the shadows, the children watched these men and women gather around their fire, open their medicine bundle, pass the pipe and offer up their prayers. That medicine bundle was, under our law, an illegal possession, and the prayers were a heathen practice to be stamped out. Whenever the children were discovered, they were shooed away, not because the Elders wished to exclude them but because they didn't want the children to come to grief with us.

Fifty years later, that man was still trying to discover the cultural roots denied him as a child. He had been taken off to a residential school on the prairies at the age of six, had been baptised in the Catholic church, married, gone to teacher's college, begun teaching, then fallen prey to alcoholism. For a time he lived in the ditches at the edges of our cities. He finally came to himself and began to search for his history, for his real people and for his traditional values. Like many other "rediscoverers" from this part of Ontario, he had to turn to the Cree of northern Alberta, since traditional thought and practices had been virtually eliminated here. He, and many others like him, have been succeeding in that quest, helping to restore their communities and themselves. Bit by bit they are becoming, to use their own words, "whole" again, and they are teaching the traditional route to that wholeness to others. It is not yet clear how their communities will choose to employ them, how their Indian-ness will find integration into communities changed in so many ways.

I recall, for instance, being impressed in one community with the fact that they had invited some prairie Cree to guide them in

✦

the construction and proper use of a sweat lodge, and that some of the youngsters were now taking part in the ceremonies. I mentioned that to the Chief in another community, indicating that I would be happy to put him in touch with people who might be of assistance if he chose to explore such things himself. He laughed somewhat ruefully, shaking his head in quiet frustration. He told me that he had invited a medicine man into the community some four years earlier for exactly that purpose. Within two days the leaders of the four mainstream churches in the community, all Native lay preachers, had threatened to have him unseated as Chief if he didn't immediately tell that "heathen" to leave the reserve. (He went on to point out that if the congregation lists claimed by those four churches were added together they would yield a number three times greater than the total reserve population; the "hunt for souls", as he put it, was still flourishing, only now it was Native preachers who were doing it.)

I suggest that we must do our best to recognize that in this period of profound readjustment we cannot expect either consensus or consistency. There simply has not been enough time for a genuine social consensus to emerge. We will undoubtedly know times when we feel ourselves wanting to scream "Make up your minds and let's get *on* with this!" but we have to remember that in many communities people are faced with the necessity of making up their minds anew about almost everything in life. Our ignorance of the scope of their challenge does not help matters. It not only tempts us to be impatient, but it also keeps us from realizing that it might help if we tried harder to explain ourselves to them.

We should, I suggest, assume this burden of explanation not so that they can necessarily adopt our ways, but so that they can have an easier time understanding and *adapting* to them. The fact that our intrusive society is here to stay does not demand the former, but it certainly demands the latter. For their part, Native people face the double challenge of rediscovering who they once were and then trying to adapt that to the reality of where they are now. These are daunting tasks, but it is clear to me that they are being undertaken with great determination by communities across the country.

✦

I must add one further anecdote related by the man I referred to above who was trying to rediscover his traditional roots. He told me that at the age of ten, when he was at residential school on the prairies, a teacher asked him what "kind" of Indian he was. His befuddled answer was "I don't know ... a good Indian, I guess." He had to write home to find out that there were many different tribal groups, and that his was Ojibway. More recently, despite his baptism in one of "our" churches, he has begun filling out that little box on forms that request information about one's religion with the initials B.A.P., for Born-Again Pagan. The gentleness and humour with which he tells his stories of personal and cultural trauma are themselves inspirational, and proof beyond doubt that he is finding great personal strength in his people's traditional culture and spirituality. I suggest that we have every reason to wish him, and the hundreds of others walking beside him on their road to rediscovery, nothing but success. Anyone who has been privileged to meet Native Elders regularly comes away from such meetings enriched in some fundamental way that defies words. Our own world, in my view, has a dire need of whatever it is that such people come to possess, and always stand ready to share.

C. THE INDIAN FAMILY

To convey what I mean by "the Indian family", I would like to examine what is involved in coming in off the trapline and, with good fortune, getting one of the few jobs available in the community. We tend to think of this as a relatively simple adjustment, one which only involves trading in some traps and snowshoes for a road-grader or a hammer and saw. Once again, we fail to see the reality.

Wage work is done for money, not the immediate personal reward of a warm fire, a hot meal, a softer bed or a warmer coat. It is done by the clock, regardless of season, weather, energy or will. It requires each person to perform a single, specialized task instead of controlling every aspect of the enterprise from start to finish. The immediate product, whether it be a graded road or a clean school washroom, rarely requires significant skill and is seldom a source of pride. The end product—money—is used to buy the same mass-produced goods everyone else has. Just as importantly, each wage-earner works beside other wage-earners instead of alongside his spouse and children.

Scarcity of wage work means that it is difficult for women to find jobs, yet they no longer have the skinning, stretching and curing of pelts which once made them essential contributors to the family's economic success. This central source of their self-esteem has disappeared. Nor do today's children develop or contribute skills essential to family maintenance. Instead, they begin to live very separate lives from their families on the reserve, lives centred around other children and non-family activities. For a significant portion of each day they are absent from their families, whether at school or out with friends. In these circumstances, the very notion of what it means to be a family—a trapping family—begins to unravel.

We must realize that there simply are not enough jobs to go around on northern reserves, even when short-term, government-funded jobs are taken into account. There is not now, and never has been, an economic *raison d'etre* for these communities outside of trapping. They never *existed* as communities until we created them. The families that once expended formidable daily effort just to survive now have virtually nothing to do, nothing to accomplish, nothing to find satisfaction in. On the typical northern reserve people live on welfare, in band-supplied housing, shop at a band store, send their children to a primary school, and use, when necessary, a nursing station. The result is a forced and numbing idleness, an idleness made less tolerable still by the fact that people now find themselves living close to many strangers, some of whom are likely to be traditionally antagonistic.

The situation of children on the northern reserves once again deserves special attention. In traditional times, the dousing of the family campfire signalled the end of each day's activity. Now it is the flicking off of the television set that signals the end of another day's boredom. In traditional times, a child's universe was peopled almost exclusively by caring relatives. Now there are dozens of other people to deal with on a daily basis, to fall in love with, fight with, oppose and befriend, all beyond the eyes and ears of

✦

concerned family members. There are the myriad opportunities for both good and harmful pursuits which larger communities provide. In many homes there are lost parents, struggling with the sudden disappearance of so many things that gave each day its significance, each person his or her sense of worth. The skills that those parents possessed are now largely unused and, just as importantly, seldom admired by the youngsters. The major formative influence in many homes has now become satellite television filling each home with wrestling matches, martial arts, urban street-gang movies and pornography. In other homes, persistent drunkenness and explosions of family violence have become both the norm and, sadly, the model which children learn to emulate.

Many parents acknowledge that their greatest frustration flows from an inability to know what, as parents, they should be doing to bring up their youngsters in a more productive fashion. In traditional times, as earlier discussed, loving children meant leaving them to learn by themselves the lessons that might carry them successfully through life. Those lessons came under the watchful eyes of family members who took care to ensure that life-threatening dangers were avoided. They tolerated lesser dangers if only because they thought that learning the hard way was the best way to learn well. There were few possibilities for violence from others, for the simple reason that for most of the year there weren't any others around.

The situation on today's reserves is not comparable. Although the dangers presented by contact with these numerous other strangers may not be life-threatening, they are dangers nonetheless, situations for which advance guidance is required. Advance guidance, of course, is exactly what the traditional ethic of non-interference specifically forbids.

Part of each parent's problem thus lies in the fact that today's reserve communities present an enlarged scope for their children to get into trouble. Another part is that parents are often ignorant of these activities, simply because their children are out on their own all day or, as is too often the case, all night. A third factor is that the most common *kinds* of dangers do not seem, at least at first blush, to be that dangerous at all. As long as a child survives, does it really matter that he or she learn by making errors that "only" result in dropping out of school, acquiring a criminal record, or developing a dependency on alcohol? To us, such things amount to critical impediments to the promise of a successful future. To a people for whom bare physical survival was the central preoccupation for thousands of years, such "minor" matters were apparently seen, at least initially, as akin to "lessons learned the hard way". Even when parents begin to view these activities in a more serious light, however, there are still a number of barriers forbidding effective response.

In the first place, family-centred groups had never before *seen* the need to establish sets of rules to govern behaviour for daily encounters with strangers. Even if they had foreseen such a need, the ethic of non-interference prohibited the expression of those rules in the form of advance guidance. The notion of then *enforcing* compliance with that advance guidance was even more foreign, more culturally repugnant. The ethic prohibiting the punishing or active disciplining of their children, it must be repeated, was founded on the same love and concern that prompts us to impose our will on our children at virtually every moment of the day.

In one community, for instance, the court list showed that a dozen young teenagers had been charged, at various times, with disturbing people by yelling and screaming late at night. A closer look at the facts showed that all had been sniffing gasoline at the relevant time. Some, in fact, had been standing thigh deep in water on a sand bar out in front of the community at three in the morning, substantially intoxicated from inhaling the vapour of gasoline. I had known about three other young people from a single, dysfunctional family in that community who had a history of heavy gasoline sniffing, but it appeared that the activity was spreading. I also knew that the child welfare agencies were almost powerless to remove such children if their habit was too pronounced, for no foster homes would accept them due to the danger they presented while handling gasoline and the unpredictable nature of their behaviour while intoxicated. This community has a total population of about 300, and the police indicated that around 40 of the teenagers were now sniffing gasoline and other solvents on a regular basis. In other words, a whole generation was at serious risk.

✦

Many parents were worried, and they had made complaints to the police and the Chief and council, but they were doing nothing to control their own children.

We called the youngsters into court, with their parents. I told them about another young man from another community, a man who, ten years ago, was also fifteen years old. I told them that he would not listen when people told him about the dangers of sniffing. He continued to do it. Over ten years, I explained, the gasoline ate away parts of his brain a little at a time, so slowly that he wasn't aware of it. He did not listen. I told them that he now is unable to think and does not say anything that other people can understand. I told them that he has no friends left and that he can barely feed himself. He spends his days all alone either in a hospital room or in a jail cell. His brain will never grow back. I told them that I didn't want to come back in ten years to find that they had become just like him, but that if they kept on sniffing they would end up just the same. I then turned to their parents and told then that I knew how hard it was to force their children to stop sniffing, but that they would have to. I talked about our idea of "tough love", about having to do unpleasant things now to prevent worse things from happening later. You could have heard a pin drop in that courtroom. Some of the young people were listening; two of them, however, seemed already permanently "stoned" and just stared off into space with a vacant smile. As for their parents, I have no way of knowing whether they believed my story (which was unfortunately true) or, more importantly, whether they were prompted into becoming the disciplinarians their children so badly need. All I can do is hope.

In many places, I am happy to say, times appear to be changing in this regard. Parents are beginning to see that alcohol abuse and gasoline sniffing are substantial long-term dangers. They have now seen enough examples of irreversible brain and nerve damage from sniffing solvents that they believe our warnings. They also acknowledge that dropping out of school impoverishes both the child and the community. As a result, an increasing number of parents are beginning to "interfere" in the lives of their children. For the most part, however, that interference still seems restricted to discussions and mild exhortations. Parents rarely give their children direct orders or impose punishment. They do, however, often invite the *court* to take such steps, asking that it impose such terms as curfews, mandatory school attendance, and abstinence from alcohol and solvents, together with the threat of court-ordered removal from the community if those terms are breached. I have seen parents ask the court to take their children into custody to save them from themselves, without ever having tried family discipline of their own. It is as if they know such things are necessary but cannot bring themselves to act as the instrument of coercion. The most constant lament from parents in courtrooms across the North is, "I have spoken with him, but he does not listen, so what can I do?"

In truth, it does not seem that such exhortations are very effective today. It may be that many of these children who have pieced together a borrowed culture from the television shows they watch see their parents as embarrassing anachronisms who can't even speak English and who "only know how to fish, trap and hunt". For too many children, their rebellion is clearly the result of living with parents whose drunken and violent outbursts do not demonstrate love but indifference or outright hostility. I suspect, however, that something more difficult to deal with is at work, for I see the same rebellion from children of sober, caring and hard-working traditional parents. I suspect the overwhelming impact of television.

To demonstrate the overt negative lessons of television, I need only mention the story line of a television movie I saw one night on a northern reserve. I had finished court and was over-nighting in the community at the police quarters. After supper I turned on the television set. There is no in-home control over channel selection in most northern reserve communities; instead, the signal comes from the satellite to the community dish where the person who operates the dish gets to select the program that everyone in the community must watch. The movie the operator selected that night told the story of a teenage girl who took slow revenge on an entire Los Angeles gang of thugs who had brutally raped and killed her younger, deaf-mute sister in a school shower stall. In the penultimate scene, the heroine watched in triumphant glee as the gang leader writhed in agony, both of his

✦

knees pierced by steel arrows, his genitals sliced away by a Bowie knife, his legs broken in Hollywood's version of a bear trap, and his body covered in flammable paste, then set afire. The flames framed the girl's satisfied smile as the sound of police sirens grew in the background. The last scene, however, did not involve the lawyers, judges, courtrooms or jails of real life. It showed the heroine at her little sister's grave, apparently free from prosecution and surrounded by supportive girlfriends, one of whom said something like "It's okay, so-and-so, you made it right."

I cannot help but wonder if children living four hundred air miles north of Thunder Bay think they are seeing what life is really like in Los Angeles or New York when they watch this sort of fare. If they do, then they have good reason to be mystified when they are hauled in front of a judge for breaking a window at school or stealing potato chips from the community store.

It is clear that whatever expectations these children may have of life in large cities, they often imitate, out of boredom or frustration or anger, what they watch on television. A number of reserves are plagued by youth gangs wearing costumes identical to those seen on TV, right down to leather, studs and nanchuka sticks. Longstanding intra-family animosities help to inflame the wars between different gangs, and empty, jobless days offer no alternative to the mindless violence. I know of one youngster who needed over fifty stitches to close a ritual cross carved into his chest as an initiation rite into one of the gangs. In another case, an elderly couple were tied to chairs and burned with cigarettes in a vain effort to get them to hand over alcohol they didn't possess. In both of these incidents, the children involved were directly imitating movies they had seen on their televisions.

I believe, however, that television is doing something even more profound to these children, and I am referring here to its McLuhanesque impact on Native culture. It is not only the plot lines which "teach"; of even greater influence is the fact that they implicitly teach what whites have learned as the proper ways to relate to ourselves and to each other. Our television cannot help but teach our fundamental rules: it shows us expressing our emotions, talking out our griefs and sorrows, expressing our worries and concerns to all who might wish to hear them (and to many

✦

who don't), constantly offering advice and criticism, demonstrating anger and hostility, defining ourselves as individuals first and members of groups second. Those Indian children (and there are thousands) who spend their pre-school years parked all day in front of a television set are learning, quite simply, to be us. Then, when they go to school, they see the same kind of conduct from their white teachers. They see it from their white nurses and doctors and from white lawyers, judges, police and probation officers. The only people they do not see act in such ways are their parents and Elders.

I wonder how these children view their parents and Elders. Do the older people appear as reserved, undemonstrative, impassive and "removed" to them as they once did to me? Are parental refusals to advise and criticize seen by their children as signals of respect or of indifference? By the same token, when parents complain that their children no longer behave respectfully, is it because those children have learned through television to criticize, complain and show their anger, precisely the kinds of actions which would have been taken as intentional signals of disrespect in traditional times? And when Indian parents do not respond with the same "exaggerated" demonstrations of feeling as television parents do, do their children conclude that it signals an absence of concern?

Are these children and their traditional parents separated by a generation gap of 20, or of 2,000 years?

At the same time, there is another group of parents in each community who experience yet another set of problems. They are the group that, as children, spent the major portion of each year in a residential school. As these people are the first to acknowledge, they came out of those schools with hardly any knowledge of family life. They had no role models for parenting except their teachers, and their experience during childhood was not of a laissez-faire environment but of rigid discipline, often coupled with corporal punishment. They did not experience any sort of reciprocal give-and-take between adults and children, any sort of day-to-day building of *family* dynamics. The people in this group are especially at a loss when it comes to raising their children, because they have *no* known family model to follow. They observe traditional parents letting children make almost all of their own choices without comment, and they contrast that with the regimented, pseudo-military experience of their boarding schools. The result is that they feel torn in two opposite directions. Those who follow the strict disciplinary approach of the residential schools often meet with strong disapproval from their more traditional peers; their children, quite naturally, complain loudly about how much freedom those other children have. Lacking a clear, family-based precedent in their own experience, these parents switch back and forth between the two extremes, confusing both their children and themselves. The result is a mixture of inconsistency and uncertainty, an unfortunate combination in any context and especially so in the context of child-rearing.

It is little wonder that open-ended surveys of the social needs identified by adults in reserve communities in northwestern Ontario most frequently show "parenting skills" at the top of the list. Parents are very aware that their children are increasingly at risk but that they don't yet have any solid notion of the most appropriate way to respond. Again, there is no new consensus, and the struggle to find one is taxing the best efforts of all.

It is undeniable that most Native families in the remote communities are not what they were as recently as twenty or thirty years ago. For parents, there are few sources of self-esteem outside the family, and a greatly diminished scope for influence within it. Their children are rebellious, spurred into self-destructive habits by what they watch on their television sets and by the vision of a future of idle days devoid of opportunity for self-fulfilment. Although women still retain the rewards of motherhood, their scope for achievement and contribution has been dramatically reduced. Children hear of their duty to respect parents and Elders, but too frequently see nothing they consider worthy of respect. Parents feel they are inadequate to the parenting task facing them, either because traditional practices no longer seem to secure their children from harm or because growing up in residential schools left them with no family model to follow. For both kinds of parents, the abstract idea of the family seems to find little correspondence with the reality of their own families, and they are

✦

at a loss over what to do. Their worry about the future—for their children and their communities—and their esteem-destroying suspicion that the failure is theirs, have a corrosive effect on individual and community mental health.

Given what has occurred in these communities over the course of the last twenty or thirty years, no one should be surprised that there is significant social chaos in many of them today. In fact, our response should instead be one of admiration, for despite the terrible hurdles these people face every day, they retain a fierce determination to prevail and to rediscover an equilibrium within the family context. Even though my professional work submerges me in all of the dysfunctions that exist in those families, my over-riding emotional response has been one of admiration for the strength I have witnessed. Despite almost overwhelming odds, they have neither given up nor given in.

In fact, there are many signs that the tide is turning now that they are beginning to voice their confusion, seek help and bring their creative energies to bear. As I've suggested in other contexts, their challenge now involves an almost complete redesign of community-approved approaches. This amounts, in many communities, to an overt and deliberate process involving workshops on parenting, complete with outside consultants, both Native and non-Native. At one such workshop, the question being asked was how far parents could go in the physical discipline of their children without being charged with assault. Everything is now up for grabs, and once again it will be fascinating to watch the struggles for new approaches and techniques. Once again, our response should be characterized both by patience and by a readiness to join in, to support the discussions whenever our contributions are sought.

D. CERTAINTY IN A NATIVE CONTINUUM

I spoke earlier of the notion of a circular track or path of existence, and about how central that notion was to Native visions of the past, present and future. The primary duty of each generation was to prepare the next for its turn on the path, to see the baton successfully transferred and to ensure that the journey was as sustaining for them as it had been for their predecessors. I spoke of the security which such a definition of life would provide, the security of believing in an ordered and certain continuum.

It is my guess that the remote northern communities sense that this vision, this conviction, is slipping away and that in this critical respect the *ordering of life* is slipping away with it. I sense a fear that life itself, Indian life, is seen as threatened by an escalating process of disintegration.

I am not referring to the obvious social disintegration which alcohol abuse, violence and family dysfunction cause, for in many ways these are only symptoms of the more fundamental kind of falling apart I wish to address here. The disintegration I point to is the one which is feared by even the most peaceful and ordered of the remote communities. To put it plainly, the fear is that young people will choose to leave. Many already have. The repercussions for "Indian-ness" may be far more substantial than any outsider can anticipate.

Should the majority of young people choose to strike off on their own, to make their solitary ways in our post-industrial world, it will mean the end of many things, physical and spiritual, that have always been central to Indian life. Families will no longer be Indian families, with all their living generations in close proximity, together in mind, spirit and body, inter-protective and nourishing. Without the extended family, the central duty to dedicate one's self to the welfare and continuance of the group will also be gone. Gone too will be the parents' ability to teach by example all that their children will need to lead successful lives by *anyone's* definition. Nor will parents be able to find comfort in the belief that they have equipped their children adequately for the future. Instead, parents will pass their days in impotent concern as their children move into wholly unfamiliar contexts. Although we too face this concern as parents, we have both accustomed ourselves to it and have deliberately taught our children to be autonomous. We no longer perceive their departure into independent lives as an unnatural loss; it is, in fact, what we have dedicated ourselves to as the appropriate result of growing up.

✦

There is also the concern that the Native communities of the North will physically disappear over time. For a people who strongly relied upon particular tracts of land to help form both individual and group identities, the very thought of leaving those landscapes empty after so many generations seems like a betrayal of that past and of the people who lived it. At the same time, I think there is a fear among the older people that whoever does desert the ancestral home will find *himself* suddenly empty, removed from the strengths of the past, cut off from the wisdom and guidance of those who went before. The young people who have not come to know the terrain in this spiritual way may not have this fear, but I sense it in the eyes of their Elders. They fear not only the physical end of the community itself but also the resulting impoverishment of each individual who goes off alone into our cities of concrete and steel. The unspoken concern seems to be, "If you leave, you are lost not only to us but to yourself as well."

I remember one father whose son had to appear in court. He wanted to take his son off with him to the trapline again. The purpose, he explained, was not so that his son could also become a trapper and live as he had. Instead, it was so he could "find" himself, find out "who he was" and "what strengths are within him". If he found those things, his father said, the boy would be better able to withstand all of the pressures he would find when he left the community to make his way "in your world".

This is a much greater problem for the northern bands than for their counterparts in the south. Practically every decision made by remote northern bands and by individual members of those bands is influenced by one haunting question: how will this decision affect the survival of my community and my family's future? Will they survive at all, or will everything my ancestors believed in and knew cease to exist?

The people living on less remote reserves, especially those connected by road to nearby urban locations, enjoy a luxury unknown to their northern counterparts. They are able to participate, selectively, in the educational, occupational, recreational, and social opportunities of those urban locations on a daily basis, returning each night to their Indian homes. They can choose to have as little or as much involvement with us as they please.

✦

For the residents of the remote reserves, however, the luxury of selective and careful involvement does not exist. Anyone who wishes to participate in outside opportunities has to leave home completely, often for very long periods of time. Underlying every choice about participation in our world, then, is the deeply troubling question of whether the person who goes away will ever come back. Everyone who climbs aboard an aircraft to go off to school or a job in the south constitutes a threat to the survival of their community, for if he or she does not return, then the human resources of that community have been depleted. The smaller communities feel each such departure with great pain, for they have not only lost that one person but also the generations of children that will issue from them.

The degree to which each individual is concerned about the impact of his or her departure upon both the fate of the community and the Indian sense of family continuity cannot be overestimated. Each person raised on a remote reserve is brought up to feel a personal obligation to contribute to the perpetuation of the home community and of its sustaining vision. This is the conviction that underlies the ambivalence many parents feel about sending their youngsters away to continue their schooling. Just as importantly, it gnaws at the hearts of those who do go out. Natives are a communal people for whom group and family loyalties used to override all other concerns. They raised their children not to leave but to stay forever, to wear their old clothes, take over their tasks and conceive new generations to be, as Dr. Brant phrased it, "layered" onto the family. Personal worth was evaluated in terms of the roles one played within the continuing family, not in terms of individual's operating autonomously, selfishly, within a larger society. So strong and common is this notion among Native peoples across the continent that the greatest way for a Navajo to praise another person is to say, "He takes care of his relatives." Whereas whites praise parents who raise their children to be autonomous, such parents would have been failures judged by traditional Native standards. It is, in my view, this sense of family obligation which, more than any other factor, makes it so hard for Native people to settle happily into our towns and cities. Certainly they face other obstacles as well, including language skills, job-training, new rules governing interpersonal behaviour, and overt racism. They are also, without doubt, exceedingly lonely. I suspect, however, that the most significant obstacle to successful transition into our urban life is one we seldom guess at: *guilt*, guilt over leaving their family and their community. Why would we guess at it, when leaving home is what we believe we are supposed to do?

As with the sheer sense of loss discussed just above, this sense of guilt, of desertion, may be much more pronounced in Native people from the remote reserves. A stronger adherence, perhaps, to traditional notions of group and family loyalty may be a part of it. The more critical reason, however, may come from the inescapable fact that their communities have a more desperate need of their contributions. A community of several hundred or even a thousand people deep in the bush cannot afford to lose its most promising youth to the cities. It needs every bit of energy, enthusiasm, talent, skill and dedication it can find just to keep essential services intact. This knowledge of their community's need, I suspect, is a source of agony for every person who leaves. "What am I doing?" they ask, "What kind of person am I, out here working just for myself when my family and my community are in such need of me?"

There are many stories of Native people from the North who, after they have secured good jobs and homes and friends in the city, suddenly pack it in and go home. No one seems to understand why. Why leave what one fought so hard to gain, why go back to poor housing, inferior schooling and the possibility of welfare subsistence? At our most charitable, we attribute such returns to loneliness. At our least charitable, we attribute them to an inability to "make it" in the real world or, worse still, to simple indolence. We don't very often see the degree to which their sense of responsibility—and the feeling that they have betrayed that responsibility—overwhelms them.

Unfortunately for many who do return, they do so changed in many ways that their families and communities have a hard time accepting. To succeed in our schools and jobs, they have had to adopt many of our self-assertive and interventionist ways. They have had to adopt our impatience, our preoccupation with the time-clock and deadlines, and our belief that consensus is unessential to corporate decision-making. In short, judged by traditional standards, they no longer behave as Indians ought to behave. As a result, they are often viewed with suspicion when they return to become involved in band life. They frequently fall into a sort of no man's land; they alternate between periods of active, frequently resented, community involvement and wholesale, often bitter, retreat. There are, of course, many who return and jump into band life with a vigour that cannot be defeated, and these people deserve our respect for their determination and commitment. They also deserve our patience, for they cannot act with the same speed they might have demonstrated in the urban setting. They have many constituencies to please among their own people. Given the central requirement of consensus, they must walk slowly and tread softly, especially where the community is composed of families who have no history of close cooperation. Many Native leaders, we must recall, are asking their own people to consider discarding notions of propriety that have been inviolable for thousands of years. They are not helped in their task by our unreasonable impatience.

We must remember that within the context of their long-established notions of what is proper, the things which our world offers come with significant price tags. By going to our schools, children may become better equipped to master our economic realities, but in the process they may also un-learn a morality that traditionally forbade cultivating individual egos through competition, praise, comparison, censure, reward and punishment. Leaving the community to take up positions in tribal councils or native-run child welfare agencies may well assist in the delivery of more culturally-sensitive services to those who remain, but it still results in a drain of necessary talent away from the community.

Most people are not aware of the immense responsibilities borne by each Chief and council, responsibilities which would never be imposed on the municipal councils of our towns and cities. All housing on northern reserves is band-built, requiring that councils perform needs-assessments and then submit funding applications to government. Virtually all building on the reserves is done by band members under the ultimate direction of band

✦

council, often acting as general contractor. No one owns a house privately, with the result that councils have to allocate houses among band members, choosing who succeeds and who fails to get a house of their own. With housing in such short supply, many people are left with no alternative but to stay with their families even as they have children of their own, and they regularly hold council to blame. The administration of welfare, a regretably large undertaking, is also under band control. With growing band supervision of education, they now frequently control the hiring and firing of teachers, the development of curricula, the purchase of supplies and the maintenance of the school buildings. Given the state of social disruption in many communities, they also hire and supervise band police constables to help maintain the peace. In many communities there are band-supervised mental health workers, community health representatives, family service workers, youth workers, probation aides and drug and alcohol addiction counsellors. Even the supervision of court-ordered community sevice work falls to the council. Most importantly, the absence of any tax base whatever requires that Chief and council spend a major portion of each year simply lobbying the federal and provincial governments for necessary funds, whether they are needed for road maintenance, schooling, fire services, or the purchase of new office equipment for the band hall.

The council's workload is not lessened by the fact that in many of their lobbying efforts they have to deal with bureaucrats whose ignorance of the North is extremely frustrating. I recall a band manager shaking his head in disbelief as he came out of one such meeting with government officials, asking out loud why he had to go through the same "foolishness" every year. The meeting was about funding for the annual winter road (a "roadway" built and maintained for a few short months across frozen lakes and through the bush, often for a hundred miles or more, primarily to permit tractor trains to bring in construction material, but also to permit people to bring in private cars and trucks as well). The job requires heavy construction machinery to plow the road open and keep it that way, machinery which must remain running twenty-four hours a day to prevent its oil from freezing solid at temperatures of –50 degrees Fahrenheit. The officials who had prepared the budget for the winter road had once again forgotten about the need for adequate fuel for *continuous* running and, once again, had costed that fuel at southern Ontario prices, not the much higher prices which apply so far north. They had been making those same mistakes, the band manager sighed, for ten years, causing the band to repeatedly waste valuable time trying to educate them all over again.

I cannot fail to mention one of the most humorous such displays of ignorance. It was felt by one government official in Toronto that it would be wise to seek an alternative to taking problem children out of the community, especially where it was their parents who were largely responsible for their misbehaviour by not having provided adequate supervision and direction. A proposal was made to explore ways to have those children temporarily placed with more stable families in the community. Recognizing that housing is in short supply, it was suggested that such families would need some help to expand their living accommodation before they could take in anyone new. So far, so good. The proposal that was made, however, involved prefabricating small units suitable for housing the youngsters, then flying them into the appropriate communities and joining them up to existing housing. Those prefabricated additions were to be fully furnished, right down to their own toilets, sinks and bathtubs. The official who drafted the proposal was clearly not aware that there are no water and sewer systems in these communities; *no one* has a toilet, sink or bathtub as we know it. Water is either carried in by pail, or delivered by pumper truck to be stored in large, galvanized tanks, then ladled out as needed. I was tempted to keep quiet and to try my best to be quietly present when the first prefabricated unit was sky-lifted (presumably by Hercules helicopter) over three hundred miles of wilderness, gently settled in behind one of the existing homes, and then hooked up to... nothing! Taxpayer that I am, however, I helped to make certain that the architects of the proposal were suitably enlightened.

The amount of administrative and other talent it takes to apply for, create and then maintain essential services in small reserve communities is, in a word, staggering. The same few

◆

councillors must be the school board, the police commission, the welfare office, the housing authority, the social services agencies *and* the provider of virtually all jobs. If our municipal politicians ever had their duties expanded to such a degree there would be resignations everywhere. Yet even in communities as small as three hundred people, that is the load borne by band councils.

It is therefore clear that community survival requires that young people remain, for their contributions are essential. By the same token, it is not hard to see that those who have left are aware that their communities need them. When they respond to that awareness by returning, it may indicate not indolence or defeat but allegiance to traditional ethics requiring that people deny individual drives and self-interest. The desire to return home may also flow from a conviction that retracing established family, community and spiritual circles may be more rewarding and less destructive than racing hell-bent-for-leather over the urban landscape in pursuit of material fortune or fifteen-minute fame.

Whatever vision of the purpose of existence may be preferable—their traditional round-the-track relay race, or our cross-country marathon into unknown tomorrows—the fact remains that the two visions are fundamentally at odds with each other. Many Native people see their way of life threatened by virtually all contacts with our society. Reactions to that perceived conflict vary from confusion, to anger, to despair. While some Native people conclude that gaining our education is the only route to survival, others argue that the result will be survival not as Indians at all, but as copies of us. No matter what direction is ultimately chosen, what has unquestionably been lost for the moment is the security and comfort that a shared and unchallenged vision once held for everyone. Today there is instead a large measure of uncertainty, disagreement and fear, fed by a concern that the circle may be irreparably broken already, the future nothing but a question mark.

E. THE THREAT OF STARVATION

It is hard to imagine anyone bemoaning the fact that starvation is no longer a daily threat; certainly that is not my intention here. It

✦

does not follow, however, that the removal of this threat has been of little consequence. To the contrary, such an important element of traditional life could not disappear without having a profound effect upon how the society structures itself. In fact, I suspect that a great number of problems now so visible in the North owe their intractability to the disappearance of the threat of starvation.

Death by starvation was formerly one of the most powerful and cohesive forces in Native life. We have probably all heard stories of the aged and infirm walking voluntarily off into blizzards to die when food was in short supply, thereby giving the younger generation a better chance to survive. There was even an early Kenora court case where a mad woman's family was forced to kill her because her ravings were frightening away the game that they needed to survive. Even though we know of such stories, I am certain that we do not understand how controlling that fear of starvation was.

The Ojibway language itself provides a clue, for I am told that there is no equivalent to our word for "savings". There is, however, an equivalent to our word for "hoarding", complete with all its negative implications. It appears that in traditional times personal accumulation could only signal one thing: a threat to the survival of others. Even the conceptual possibility of benign personal accumulation did not exist, so thin was the margin for survival.

Recall Dr. Brant's view that ethics barring interference and the indulgence of disruptive emotions owed their existence to the need for cooperation and putting forth one's best efforts. If even constructive advice posed a risk to continued cooperation, it is clear how essential and delicately founded that cooperation was. There simply was no room for taking chances.

Of interest here is the fascinating and seemingly contradictory fact that the most central of all the rules—the one that barred interference in the free choices of others—seems to suggest that there were *no rules at all* for constraining behaviour. A highly structured society was able to maintain that structure, yet deny, to itself as well as others, that it possessed any rules for telling people what they could and could not do.

In my court work, I have had to face this apparent contradiction regularly. I hear continual complaints about the court, our

✦

instrument of rule-enforcement, when it resorts to punishment for violations of the rules. "We never punished" is the oft-repeated claim. "We talked to people instead, showed them the proper way to live, encouraged and aided them. If things finally became completely intolerable, such people might be banished. But we never punished."

I have found this apparent lack of coercion to be extremely admirable. I have also found myself wondering how it was that their traditional rules were so regularly respected that coercion, threats and punishment were never required. Were they so much more respectful of each other than we are that there was never a need to create instruments and techniques of rule enforcement?

What I may have failed to take into account is that there was such an enforcement mechanism, one whose coercive power kept everyone in line, following the rules and respecting the commandments: the threat of starvation. It was not, however, a mechanism made or supervised by man. If people stepped out of line, if they failed in their obligations of effort and excellence, they faced the immediate and occasionally fatal response of nature. The fiction could grow that there were no rules, that everyone was free to say and do as they pleased, because men were seldom called upon to impose punitive measures for contravening those rules.

In a hunter-gatherer's society restricted, for the most part, to single extended families, duties that were neglected had direct consequences not upon strangers but upon loved ones. And those were the very people upon whom *you* depended for your own survival. Injury to them meant consequent injury to yourself. In that way the threat of starvation was indeed a coercive force prompting obedience to the rules, and its interventions were likely to be both swift and severe. No court would come to enquire about the reasons behind your failure, and no attorney would plead your case; consequences would simply flow, and they would affect everyone in your family.

Even the act of banishment (which was tantamount to certain death in most cases) was structured so as to give the appearance of not being imposed. Instead of taking the actual step of ordering someone to leave and never come back, the banished person was simply left behind when the group moved on. Once again there was the custom of claiming that no one did anything to anyone else; instead, they just refused to continue their support.

It is interesting to note that although institutions of rule enforcement appear to have been rare in the North, there was already a very elaborate system of tribal courts among the agricultural Mohawk when Europeans first arrived. Although Mohawk courts emphasized consensus and rehabilitation, they also did impose schemes of compensation and restitution and, when all else failed, punishment. It is my theory that the Mohawk had no choice but to develop such institutions once the development of agriculture reduced the threat of starvation. They had to create new rules to govern year-round contact between strangers and they had to devise ways of enforcing those rules on their own once the coercive force of nature was diminished.

The Native communities of the North, however, never had the time to make such a gradual adjustment, and the pronounced reluctance to enforce social rules—their own as well as ours—remains strong in many communities. The threat of starvation may have been the factor which permitted people to coexist peacefully with each other in traditional times without ever having to systematically take the repugnant step of enforcing that peace. In this way, the possibility of starvation may have ironically provided them with a luxury which we have not known for centuries, the luxury of seeing peace maintained without anyone having to assume the unhappy role of enforcer.

One very troubled community in my region provides a good example of how difficult it is for people to suddenly take on a role of active interference in the lives of others. In this community we are rarely successful in persuading Elders or community leaders to come into court and make recommendations on appropriate sentences. In private, some younger councillors will request that I ask the court to impose relatively harsh penalties for serious offenses like impaired driving or the use of firearms while intoxicated. In public, however, they will rarely take any stand at all. The older councillors will occasionally come into court, but only to speak for a totally contradictory position, requesting probation orders no matter how serious the offence. Consequently, we have had to muddle along on our own, with almost no consistent involvement from the community. At one point youth gangs formed in that community, among both boys and girls. The kids divided the reserve into territories which different gangs claimed as their exclusive domain. Weapons and uniforms became common, copied from the street gangs glorified in movies. Gang members slept all day, then drank and fought all night, completely ignoring their parents and community leaders.

Things came to a head when, in a most unusual move, a petition from a committee of "concerned citizens" asked for a meeting with the police and the Crown Attorney. About sixty people met in the gymnasium at the community school, all of them worried about their children and their community. (As it happened, they had every reason to be concerned. We learned later that while we held our meeting more than forty boys in two rival gangs staged a rare afternoon war at the other end of the reserve, complete with clubs, chains, nanchuka sticks and chunks of fishing-net lead hung on strings).

During the course of this meeting, two things became clear. First, the police and I had been invited not because we were thought to have answers to their problems (we didn't), but because our presence would permit opposing positions and complaints to be advanced in a less confrontational fashion. The concerned citizens felt that their Chief and council were not doing enough about the gang problem, while the Chief and council felt frustrated because they could not enlist parental involvement in controlling the youngsters. Each group felt more comfortable saying such things to us than saying them directly to the other group. As the meeting progressed with very little input from us, I felt more like a conduit than a consultant.

Second, it became clear that everyone wanted someone else to be the one to interfere. At one point, for instance, someone suggested that a major source of the problem was the easy availability of gang movies both on television and at the video section of the community co-op store. Everyone agreed that this evil influence had to be stopped in some fashion. The response initially proposed by both parents and council was to pass a bylaw banning all such movies from the community.

✦

At this point, I decided to get more involved in their discussion. I said that I too disapproved of my children being exposed to such movies, but that my response as a parent had been simply to tell them that they were not allowed to watch such movies in our home. I went on to say that I understood such interference in the choices of children might have been traditionally improper, but that in these changed and threatening circumstances perhaps the issue needed some rethinking. It was, I suggested, the only effective way to protect children from such dangerous influences. Looking about the room, I thought I saw a large number of people who appeared to be taken aback by such a proposal. I venture the guess that many parents had not ever thought of such direct and overt interference. I saw a number of people nodding thoughtfully and a number of people involved in animated conversations in Ojibway. I have no way of knowing what was being considered, but I can report that there was no more discussion about a band bylaw. Only time will tell if (and in what circumstances) parents will decide to break with tradition and to take an active role in both establishing and then enforcing rules for their children in that community.

The only certain thing at this point, in my own outsider's view, is that the practices or conditions which ensured obedience in the past are no longer effective in many communities. As the gang-war meeting illustrates, parents are trying to make up their minds about where to go in the future.

Given the significant transition most communities are now going through, the only instrument for the enforcement of rules seems to be the outside court, and we are well aware that we are not a long-term answer at all.

I should add that there are several communities in my region that *have* adopted a very interventionist stand. In fact, they proclaim a right to get involved in almost every aspect of the lives of their citizens. Chief and councillors think nothing of walking into people's homes if they are concerned that there is drinking going on. They make it a practice of inspecting all luggage and boxes coming off the planes to see if alcohol is being smuggled into the community, whether or not people oppose their searches. One community regularly sends councillors upriver a number of

✦

miles off the reserve itself to search all boats coming through a narrow set of rapids, looking once again for alcohol or drugs. When charges are laid in one such community, Chief and council regularly ask that I propose penalties to the judge, including jail, that are higher than I feel comfortable with. In the spring, they order all the youngsters out for long days to clean yards of sawdust and the other inevitable debris that comes into view as the snow melts. They even have a bylaw imposing a five hundred dollar fine for cutting down a tree within the community boundaries. There is another interventionist community in my region, however, that proclaims a similar right to interfere but does so from an almost exclusively therapeutic and rehabilitative standpoint. Here the community representatives in court insist that we focus not upon punishment but upon mental, emotional, physical and spiritual rejuvenation through counselling. Both communities are active with the court, and both appear to be relatively successful in keeping antisocial activity to a minimum.

I have no idea why some communities have chosen to adopt interventionist roles while others have not, nor do I know why there are such widely differing approaches being taken among those interventionist communities. I only know that every community is faced with the necessity of having to design its own new approaches. For this reason, every community becomes its own experiment in trying to find appropriate and productive mechanisms to ensure rule obedience, now that the threat of starvation is gone. However, the very strong resistance of most Native communities to the imposition of punishment by man upon man, no matter how it arose, stands in stark contrast to our way of doing things. What they fashion in its stead, and how well it works, will be well worth watching.

F. INTEGRATED EXISTENCE

There is, I suggest, still another conviction of loss felt in the North, one that is perhaps greater by itself than the sum of all the particular losses discussed thus far. To understand the magnitude of this particular loss, we have to remember that the various rewards or satisfactions one experienced in traditional times came on a regular basis during the course of every single day, from virtually every activity undertaken. Each family off on its own in the bush occupied at one and the same time what we would call its workplace, its home, its recreation centre, its school, its nursery, its library, its shopping centre and, most critically, its place of worship. It didn't matter where one was at any particular instant; the surroundings comprised part of all of those functions.

By contrast, we lead very compartmentalized lives. We pursue our various activities with little expectation of more than one kind of reward at any one time. There is, for most of us, no spiritual component to our recreation, no family component to our work, no learning component to our shopping, no exercise component to our worship and no laughter component to our study. Above all, there is almost no sense of awe or wonder in anything we do.

It is this integration of all the "goods" in life into each activity of every day that may be responsible for the growing use of the English word "holistic" in Indian speech. They do not, I suggest, use this word to signify a strictly abstract concept but to describe as clearly as possible a central satisfaction of traditional times, one that appears to have been largely lost in the course of one or two generations. For many Native people it may also be a description of what they believe life ought to be, and of what they see as lacking in the mainstream society.

As Native people, then, watch more and more of their own people leaving to live in towns and cities, they feel that there is an unravelling of the long-standing social configuration that made their society viable. Just as importantly, they also fear that as each person takes on more of our ways he will experience an individual unravelling as he is forced to dedicate different parts of each day to discrete and compartmentalized goals. They fear that each person will be increasingly unable to realize his or her full potential. What they fear is, really, a double disintegration, with both the group and the individual falling into an unconnected and meaningless existence.

I don't mean to suggest that those kinds of fears are necessarily conscious ones, well thought-out and formulated into specific propositions. They might be easier to deal with if they were. Instead, I suspect that they exist mostly at the emotional level, as a sense of something being "missing" from life, of a longing for the past, and a trepidation about what the future holds.

When we hear Native laments for the loss of their culture, we should also be alert to the fact that they are being voiced not only to relieve *their* feelings of sadness, but also as a kind of warning to *everyone*. They are saying, to put it bluntly, that our society is unhealthy in many ways, and that if we continue on our present path we will prevent ourselves from becoming the whole and healthy people we have the capacity to be.

I cannot help but note how frequently I hear my peers (and, for that matter, myself) lament the trade-offs we feel "forced" to make. To attain reward or satisfaction in one segment of our lives, we sacrifice rewards in others. We feel ourselves constantly being forced to give up family time for career advancement, worship time for yardwork, contemplation time for shopping and exercise time for getting the car into the muffler shop. Our most common lament is that there are not enough hours in the day. We feel that we are kept from accomplishing all the things that we somehow feel we ought to be able to accomplish. In some fundamental way we feel poorer than we think we should be, and it has little to do with finances.

What I sense many Native people (especially Elders) trying to tell us, whether by words or by simple refusals to do as we do, is that we are impoverishing ourselves by conforming to a social organization that does not permit the integration of multiple "goods" into particular activities. They balk when they observe us as a distracted and frantic society full of stress, substance abuse, broken families, violence and, worst of all, a numbing loneliness. They also see their own communities showing identical problems, and they wonder how much our influence is to blame. They do not all want to return to the trapline, but neither do they want our cars and homes and vacations if they are purchased at the cost of the personal, family and social disorder they sense we suffer from. Many Native people today are seeking ways in which the central benefits once conferred by life on the trapline can be maintained while still participating fully in our technological world. I am convinced that they understand us much more clearly than we think they do, and that they are genuinely puzzled about why, with all

✦

our wealth and power, we continue to do such harmful things to ourselves—as puzzled as we are when we watch them choose *not* to leave their impoverished, often violent communities to jump into our big and beguiling cities.

The two cultures appear to have very different definitions of the word "impoverishment". And, as usual, we have made few attempts to hear or understand theirs.

G. TRADITIONAL MECHANISMS FOR COPING

It is difficult to imagine any society coping easily or well with the shock-wave of sudden change I've tried to describe. All of the underpinnings of both individual and group life came under concerted attack. Many of the things which gave life both its order and its meaning were put out of reach, denigrated or even outlawed. In their stead, we provided or imposed our own values, approaches and institutions. When they didn't work, we took it as further proof of the incapacity of Native people to handle things themselves.

This is perhaps nowhere more true than in the context of coping with the inevitable ups and downs of life. Many outsiders point to the high levels of substance abuse, violence and community disorganization in Native communities as proof of an inability to respond effectively. As I hope to demonstrate, it is my conviction that as individuals and communities they have coped exceedingly well, given the immensity of the challenge they have faced, and, just as importantly, given what has happened to the coping mechanisms which once proved successful for them. I see the violence and despair on a daily basis, but I have seen other things as well. I have seen the maintenance of warmth, kindness, gentleness, generosity and faith despite the most extreme conditions of loss and confusion.

This chapter will conclude with a discussion of a Native belief which I sense to be the underlying source of that faith and the reason for their determined perseverance against formidable odds. It is, if I am correct, a bedrock belief which has remained strong to this day, and it may stand in direct opposition to a corresponding Judeo-Christian belief central to our social organization.

✦

Before doing that, though, I want to examine the very violent interplay between our coping mechanisms and theirs. I use the word "violent" because one of our first acts after contact was to denigrate or outlaw the very mechanisms which permitted them to cope with the traumas of life. In essence, I believe we took away much of their capacity to heal themselves. I am here referring to such practices as the pipe ceremonies, sweat-lodge ceremonies, shaking-tent ceremonies, sundances and a host of other practices which we declared heathen. I do not suggest that we always knew what we were doing. But we stamped out these traditional practices nonetheless, having no idea that we were destroying their healing institutions. The result was that a people about to face the most overwhelming social disintegration imagineable were left virtually defenceless against the anger, grief and sorrow that inevitably followed.

The defenselessness of today's Native parents puts this issue in stark relief. They feel most keenly the sorrow, confusion and pain that changed times have brought. As I have already noted, they watch their children follow dangerous, self-destructive paths and feel powerless to intervene. With memories of the recent past still alive, they sense all around them developments which threaten any clear vision of a healthy future. As the incidents of drunken violence and self-abuse which have characterized this period of social and individual confusion continue to increase, they attend the funerals and watch their youngsters being thrown into prisons far away from home. Men, once essential to family survival, have little to do but collect and spend their welfare cheques. Their feelings of futility and uselessness grow. Women too, though still buttressed by the needs of their infants, sense that their children now have comparatively little need for them and, worse still, act towards them with anything but traditional respect.

What tools do parents have to deal with all of these emotional challenges? Can they share their fears with each other? Can they express their sorrow? Can they stand up and voice their opposition and complaint? Or are those not the sorts of responses which traditional ethics expressly forbade?

Dr. Clare Brant has commented at length on the danger of improper emotional release.

✦

This "anger must not be shown" principle gives rise to a certain number of difficulties psychiatrically. For instance, it gives rise to explosiveness under the influence of alcohol. That is to say, anger that has been stored up, never shown, not ventilated and discharged, comes pouring out when the person is intoxicated. It also results, by a complicated psychological mechanism, in a high incidence of grief reactions among the Indian people. In Moose Factory we published a paper on the Moose Factory Project. We found that 44% of the people who presented themselves for psychiatric treatment at Moose Factory and in the Moose Factory Zone were suffering from a grief reaction. That is to say, they had lost a child, husband, mother or spouse and had not recovered. Some people would be grieving, I mean really grieving, crying, no appetite, not able to do the housework, five, six or ten years after the loss. . . .

Another thing that happens with this repression of anger is that one sees what is called in psychiatric jargon "pseudo-mutuality" in families and married couples. Pseudo-mutuality means emotional divorce. That is to say, people continue to live together, continue to present themselves as a couple in the community, but for all practical purposes they are divorced. They are not allowed to express their anger towards each other, but they stay together under uncomfortable circumstances.

I am trying to introduce the concept of divorce into the Moose Factory Zone as an alternative to murder. It is not cricket to divorce your husband, but if he is so aggravating that you must get rid of him, it is a better alternative to take a shotgun and blow him away some night when he is in a drunken stupor, for which you will get two years probation. But if you left him and moved in with somebody who treated you better, then you would be condemned by the community for doing that.

It is quite possible that this condemnation of divorce may not flow from traditional ethics but from those brought by the missionaries. Among the Ojibway of Lake of the Woods it appears that divorce, while not common, could have been accomplished

✦

in traditional times by the relatively painless manoeuvre of simply staying away from your tent until after the sun rose on a new day. It appears that the society which imposed severe constraints upon the expression of criticism or anger, even between spouses and even for constructive purposes, nevertheless provided a way out if those spouses could not maintain a healthy equilibrium under those constraints. It may have been the missionaries who imported the present day conviction that marriage is forever and divorce an almost cardinal sin.

Can you imagine never being able to speak about the unavoidable irritants in a marriage, never being able to unburden yourself of the sorrow of unavoidable tragedies? Imagine having to live under those constraints in today's reserve conditions of stress, trauma and loss. Imagine being culturally prohibited from expressing your fears for the future, even to your loved ones. Imagine believing, to the contrary, that it was your duty *not* to do so, but to bury those negative thoughts, to forget yesterday's tragedy, to keep it all inside where it will not burden others. Was it possible to keep it all inside in traditional times? Was the threat of starvation so great that people could in fact accomplish such feats of sublimation?

Or were there other mechanisms for relief from such disruptive emotions, other mechanisms which respected the bans against indulging and expressing them? Even the asking of such a question demonstrates how much we are prisoners of our own culture, for we have a hard time admitting that our way of dealing with such things—talking them over between ourselves—might not be the only way.

Our healing processes, at least since Jung and Freud, have concentrated upon intellectual analysis and a verbal confrontation of our internal demons. It is an intellectual as opposed to spiritual journey that we embark upon, summoning up the past to make us conscious in an intellectual way of all the causative events which lie behind our present emotional state. It is our conceit that this is the only productive method of dealing with the crippling forces within us, of restoring our personal equilibrium and inter-personal harmony.

✦

When we encounter Native people who do not take to our predominant form of healing, who refuse to open themselves up in our way, we believe we see people who are not interested in healing themselves or, worse still, who are incapable of so doing. These are the unwritten conclusions of many of the psychiatrists, psychologists and other therapists who prepare reports for our courts to assist them in finding an appropriate sentence; the message between the lines is that the Native cannot or will not help himself. In our conceit, we assume that he who doesn't choose our way is left with no way. We fail to ask the simplest of questions, such as "Do you want to turn your life around, to heal yourself?" and "If you do, how do you think such healing might best be accomplished?" In fact, the history of Native people in our jails shows that when they *have* asked to be able to bring appropriate healing measures into play we have scoffed at their requests. It is only recently that prison officials are permitting, or encouraging, Elder visitation and pipe ceremonies, sweet-grass and sweat-lodge ceremonies.

I don't believe that we have to understand how such spiritual healing works (though I will give my best guesses in the final chapter) to know *that* it works. For thousands of years of a very harsh existence Native people coped successfully with their inevitable sorrows and stresses. Not only have they survived, but, as we are slowly coming to appreciate, they retain as a people an impressive dignity and a strong sense of self-worth. It seems clear that they did not psychoanalyse themselves into that state, so there must have been other mechanisms. Why is it, then, that we so regularly fail to make the connection when we hear repeated requests for pipe ceremonies, sweat ceremonies and the like from Native people in our hospitals, jails and treatment centres? Why do we want to write those practices off as hocus pocus instead of recognizing that they have healing potential?

There is a remarkable resurgence in the use of traditional ceremonial healing not only within Native communities but within Native-run treatment centres for those with substance-abuse or other problems. Obviously, these traditional practices are not instituted to serve as tourist attractions, for there are no tourists present, only Native people in search of help from other Native people. They are instituted because they are considered appropriate and productive.

At the same time, such treatment programs also incorporate some aspects of our healing techniques, for there is an increasing focus upon talking, upon sharing grief and sorrow verbally with other loved ones, and upon disclosing the traumas of the past in an effort to finally leave them behind. From what I have seen thus far, this combination of intellectual and spiritual healing seems to be a potentially powerful tool. I have watched the most dysfunctional of families return from such centres with new insights and new faith. Part of their apparent success comes from the Native insistence that the whole family be involved, that it be a "holistic" approach which recognizes that all must know what each suffers so that all can contribute towards comfort and help instead of unwittingly contributing towards making things worse. Another part involves putting a stamp of approval on the disclosure and discussion of private feelings and past traumatic events, together with learning *how* to speak of such things. The third part involves the use of traditional ceremonies (which may *also* be new to many Native people, thanks to our efforts to eradicte them) and the capacity of those ceremonies both to "cleanse" each individual and to then prompt him or her to a solemn re-dedication towards helping other family members in need. I will deal with these notions of cleansing and re-dedication more fully in Chapter 10 when I try to give some description of my own sweat-lodge experience.

The tiny community of Muskrat Dam in northwestern Ontario, a remote village accessible only by aircraft, has recently established a family healing centre, and it is already showing very positive preliminary results. In talking with the men and women who have gone through its four-week program, I have heard encouraging things. They speak of learning about the problems of other family members, about the worries which they had not been able to share before. They also speak of how the sweat ceremony helped them to see their own family as an important thing that they now wish to make "whole" again. They speak with both a sense of relief and a sense of faith, as if they had not been able to see ways to climb out of their problems, whether they involved substance abuse, family violece, repressed trauma or fear

✦

of the future. It seems as if this treatment centre, and the others I am hearing of, are finding ways to marry our confrontational and conversational techniques to their own spiritual practices. In fact, they appear to be eliminating many of the more confrontational elements in our approaches, perhaps by including the whole family and by doing so in ways which emphasize the value of each individual to the group. I would hazard a prediction that in time many of our mainstream professionals will be studying these developments with interest. Maybe, just maybe, they will admit that there is some room for improvement in our own approaches.

This one context—helping people cope with personal trauma and apprehension—illustrates with dramatic clarity another facet of what many Native people mean when they speak of cultural genocide. A culture is, in its vulnerability, much like a house of uniquely shaped cards. Take one card away and the entire structure is threatened with collapse. Insert another person's card, shaped to fit his unique house, and it may well displace more than it supports, further weakening an already shaky structure. That outsider's card may have been designed to perform the same *function* as the missing one, but it is so uniquely tailored to fit with its complementary cards that it may prove counterproductive when jammed into another structure. If that outsider's card is to prove useful at all, it must be substantially reshaped, *a task which can only be done by its new owner*, for only that person (or culture) is fully aware of the fit that must be found. Just as importantly, that reshaping can only take place if there is adequate time for reflection and experimentation. In the North, the time has been so short and full of other stresses that one can only look on in amazement that anything remains standing at all.

At the same time as our culture effectively took away all traditional mechanisms for coping, it added a different, very seductive "coping" assistant: alcohol. People in our society lean on the bottle in the mistaken belief that it will help them deal with the stress in their lives. The frequency and extent of alcohol abuse in many Native communities, however, is of almost epidemic proportions.

Many observers have suggested that this abuse has been caused by idleness, poverty and deprivation. That may be partly accurate, at least to the extent that those factors lead to feelings of anger and frustration which have no other form of release. We know, however, that the result of introducing alcohol is frequently the same even in sub-arctic communities where oil has been discovered or where mines have suddenly appeared close enough to Native communities to provide both jobs and prosperity. The incidence of alcohol abuse and alcohol-induced violence often escalates dramatically despite relative affluence and job-filled lives. When that still happens, we move to a fall-back position, assuming that the high rates of alcohol abuse are due to a combination of cultural influences and perhaps a physiological inability to metabolize alcohol, or to use the substance in moderation.

My conjecture, however, is that the answer is far simpler than that. I suspect that Native people use alcohol in exactly the same way that many of us do: to blow off steam. Unfortunately, two unique factors come into play where Natives are concerned. The first is the obvious fact that their "steam" has reached a point of pressure that is hard for us to imagine, given all of the losses and confusions described so far. The second factor, however, may be the most critical, for it involves the fact that Native people may have been left with no other culturally sanctioned way to vent that steam. Quite clearly, their sources of sorrow, anger and personal desperation regularly exceed anything the rest of us are ever likely to experience. When, at the same time, traditional ethics forbid even expressing those sentiments and traditional methods of spiritual healing have all but been eradicated, the bottle remains almost the *only* avenue available to pursue release. Alcohol "permits" the saying and doing of things which would otherwise not be tolerated, for it permits the individual and his community the comfort of being able to say, "It wasn't really me who broke all those traditional rules and did all those immoral things; I was just drunk."

It must be acknowledged that whites are guilty of the same rationalization and behaviour. Many of us reach for alcohol when we can't handle things on our own, then try to excuse our drunken behaviour in an identical way. Imagine what role alcohol might play if we were forbidden any other form of release—conversational, religious, or ceremonial. Are we not daily bombarded with exhortations to be honest with each other, to open up and talk about what is bothering us, to "let it all hang out"? Don't millions of us watch exactly that when we tune into Geraldo Rivera or Oprah Winfrey on television? Have we not elevated psychoanalysis almost to the level of a necessity? Even with all that, as a society we still abuse alcohol in alarming proportions. If alcohol were the only apparent avenue of release, it is likely that it would become a daily refuge for many more of us, especially if our sources of grief and frustration were as extreme as they are in many Native communities.

The problem with emotional release through alcohol, of course, is that it is only temporary. The fires that caused the emotional pressures to build in the first place are not extinguished. If cultural dictates preclude their venting in other ways, those unabated pressures flare up once again, and once again only alcohol is close at hand. Another man demolishes his house with an axe, then attacks his wife. No one can pinpoint what it was that provoked him that particular night for the simple reason that "the" provocation was years of unresolved emotional turmoil. Even when asked about those long-term sources of frustration, he will be unlikely to answer, for, as Dr. Brant noted, he will have been trained not to consciously think about them, not to acknowledge or explore them. He will only know that he got drunk and, from what other people have told him, did some terrible things. That recognition too will get buried, added to the cauldron within, undetectable as long as he remains sober, but waiting to erupt again.

That dynamic, repeated in one household after another, leads to catastrophic community results. In fact, it leads to exactly the situation earlier described where one out of every ten people in one entire community stood charged with a criminal offence on a single court day.

I recall a conversation I once had with a young Native man in his early twenties. I had watched him grow up, and had guided with his father. The father had developed such a severe alcohol problem that most of his income went to drinking, with the result that his children were frequently hungry. The one son, however, was bright and determined to overcome these drawbacks. He had stayed in school much longer than his contemporaries, and when I first met him he had gotten himself a summer job as a bellhop at an exclusive tourist resort, an unusual accomplishment for a Native boy of thirteen. He was a very perceptive young man, looking hard at himself and at the world around him. In fact, one of his teachers had shown me an essay he'd written about *already* falling into the abuse of alcohol himself, at that young age. In the essay he wrote particularly of the shame he felt when he got drunk and then said or did harmful things to others. It was a shame so great that he had a difficult time facing those people again when he met them in the community. He, like many teenagers, had a hard time forgiving himself. Each new source of shame about his own behaviour then became a fresh reason to drink. He had known that, even at age thirteen, but he wrote that he couldn't find a way to stop it.

It was that issue we were speaking of one night eight or nine years later, the issue of his sense of helplessness, his inability to rectify the harm already done or to prevent himself from inflicting new harm during the course of future drinking bouts. At one point in the conversation he suddenly slammed his fist on the table and yelled, "It didn't used to be like this! Before you came we were not like this. I hate you!" Then he looked up at me and said, "But I can't hate *you*, because you didn't do it. I'm sorry." What made an indelible impression on me at that instant was both the depth of his anger and the extent of his frustration at not being able to direct it at anyone who deserved it. The inevitable result was that he turned it upon himself. He hated himself for not being able to handle himself, for letting all the things trapped inside him take control and constantly make things worse.

That conversation took place in a bar, and he was already getting drunk once again. Otherwise, he would never have told me that directly of his feelings, and he would never have spoken about hating me. Ask any bartender in the North and you will hear the same thing about Native people and drinking: they get talkative first, then loudly morose, then prone to instantaneous outbursts of rage, often accompanied by physical violence. These sudden explosions, in fact, have a name in the North. They are called "going Indian".

✦

I put forward the possibility that it is the retention of ethics prohibiting complaint, advice and the expression of anger and sorrow, which help make alcohol so important an influence on northern reserves, especially when those prohibitions are accompanied by the absence of traditional mechanisms for self-restoration.

One smaller reserve in my region provides some support for that hypothesis. For many years it was a place of terror, with alcohol abuse leading to extreme violence, including multiple suicides, on a regular basis. Over the past several years a significant proportion of the adult population has gone out to Native alcohol treatment centres for month-long programs. On many occasions, both spouses went together. The violence has now largely stopped. At first glance, credit for that change goes to the program that convinced those people of the dangers of alcohol abuse. Closer inspection, however, suggests that the real impact of the program probably flowed from its focus upon the necessity of communicating the things that trouble people in their everyday lives. Native people at that treatment centre were teaching other Native people how to express their emotions , how to articulate their concerns and how to ask for (and give) assistance. It is my view that what they learned about the dangers of alcohol was secondary to the instruction they received on how to effect an emotional resolution.

This conclusion is also supported by the between-the-lines content of a very moving speech given by the Chief of the Alkalai Lake Band to the Whitehorse conference I referred to earlier. In explaining how his British Columbia community turned itself around, he too spoke about alcohol counselling. His more pointed exhortations, however, were to "speak from the heart to one another," to "share your feelings, your concerns," and to "open up your hearts and share your troubles." As I listened, I did so first as a white man would. I found his message of sharing and love very touching, but far from earth shattering. But when I tried to listen while keeping Dr. Brant's description of traditional ethics in mind, I was able to appreciate how radical his message really was. He was asking for nothing less that an abandonment of some centuries-old commandments. He was telling his Native

✦

audience to speak of their anger and grief, not to bury them. He was telling them to reach out to advise others, to offer them constructive criticism, to interfere. It should be noted that the Alkalai Lake Band is being studied and emulated in Native communities across the continent because of their remarkable self-recovery.

As the people of Alkalai Lake brought their substance abuse under control, the talking brought out a deeper problem: intergenerational histories of sexual abuse. That issue, too, is being treated in the same way, through community-instigated disclosure and discussion. In fact, the Alkalai Lake Reserve has become an acknowledged leader in the field of community healing, primarily because the people there consciously chose to move away from hiding and burying their grief and anger.

Their example is being closely examined by Native communities in my own region. I recently attended a two-day series of workshops examining the sexual abuse of children at a reserve close to Kenora. It was sponsored by the band council and the community education authority. They have taken on the task of trying to convince community members that silence is their first enemy. They went so far as to record the workshops on video camera and then broadcast them into each home in the community. I expect a number of other reserves in this region to take similar steps over the next several years.

How those communities which begin to face up to histories of sexual abuse decide to respond to such disclosure is another issue entirely. If they choose to pursue them through the criminal justice system, my system, then the end result will be substantial numbers of people serving long periods of time in jail. I doubt very much that this is the route they will want to pursue. Instead, I foresee them following the Alkalai Lake example once again and treating the process of disclosure as an opportunity for healing rather than for the prosecution of criminal acts. Alkalai Lake did not involve the criminal courts in handling this issue; instead, they built a healing lodge for victims and abusers alike, concentrating upon honesty, forgiveness and treatment. It remains to be seen how the white criminal justice system, with its emphasis on the jailing of sexual offenders, will choose to

✦

respond to the preferences of Native communities in my region as disclosure increases.

I suggest that what all of us from the outside *must* do is assist any community that wants to begin the painful process of learning how to honestly speak to itself. We can fund efforts by those communities to have other Native people attend to share their experiences of abuse and of healing. We can recognize the role that traditional ceremonial healing can play, and help fund the attendance of Elders to instruct communities in practices that have been lost. We can use our information base to bring knowledge of the efforts which other communities have made, and we can provide funding for the construction and maintenance of Native healing centres. Until such things are accomplished, it is my fear that alcohol will continue to be the only recourse available to many thousands of people, and the violence and despair will continue to mount. We can also encourage our own jails and hospitals to involve Native healers and to provide support for their preferred ways of treatment, whether or not we have any understanding of how they actually work. Native people are not asking *us* to adopt sweat lodges and sweet-grass ceremonies; they are only asking that we permit them to choose what might be most effective for them. In all probability what they settle on will be an interesting combination of their traditional ways and our modern ones. This kind of synthesis is only just beginning, but it is making itself felt right across the country.

I further suspect that the movement towards community-initiated disclosure and community-designed healing, especially in the context of sexual abuse, will get at the roots of such problems far faster than we will in our large towns and cities. Native communities may be able to mount such campaigns effectively partly because they are small, but also because there exists a strong belief that each individual bears responsibility for the health of the group. If ethics that once demanded personal submission to the needs of the family can be extended from the single-family context into the multi-family, community context—and perhaps beyond—then progress may be rapid. That challenge is the subject of the final segment of this chapter.

H. THE FAMILY-CENTRED IN-GROUP

Every social group creates rules to govern relations between members of that group, rules which may be entirely ignored when dealing with others. Traditional Native rules, as indicated, were designed within the context of a special group: one's own extended family. The further one got from that family, the more the gloves could come off.

In the small village north of Kenora where I worked for eleven years as a fishing guide, there were three major extended-family groups in the Native population. In 1968 they each occupied the land around a different bay, and they did not get along. The members of each family usually guided for different tourist camps, a fact I was not conscious of until I became head guide at the largest fishing lodge in the area. Wanting to create the best guide corps possible, I sought out the most skilled guides I could find from each of the families and encouraged them to come to work for me. As it turned out, I was setting up a turf war. One night on my way home I walked past a rock outcrop to see the leaders of two of the families squaring off, silhouetted (as it happened) against a beautiful sunset. One was short, stocky, and incredibly strong. The other, by contrast, was tall, lanky and deceptively quick. The latter took one long, arcing swing of his arm, caught the former squarely under his chin, laid him out cold, then calmly walked away. When I told the story to some of my more experienced friends, they laughed. "Oh, that's just those two families," they said.

I began to watch more closely, and found signs of the rivalry everywhere. If four men from one family showed up to guide but only one from the other, the outnumbered one would just disappear. At shore lunches, members of different families would eat in their own cluster well away from the others, and there was virtually no communication or cooperation between them. After a while I adjusted, making certain never to mix families together when setting up multi-boat fishing parties.

This pattern was more starkly revealed when some young men from a reserve fifty miles up the road came looking for work. They lasted one day. The police told me that the local men had given them a good beating and told them never to come back. They didn't.

The same desire to keep clear of other family groups continued when, in the early 1970s, the Ontario government decided to build a number of new homes within the village. The traditional bays were some distance from the village itself, making it very difficult for children to get to school, and difficult as well for the government to deliver adequate health and other services. As luck would have it (because I don't believe the government people had the slightest awareness of local history), there were four open parcels of land in the townsite, with the result that four clusters of new homes were built, each distant from the others. The families by and large occupied those sites along family lines, leaving only the lodges, stores, businesses and bars as places of friction.

The identical dynamic exists on virtually every reserve in my region. Inter-family mistrust in some locations is so pronounced that the federal Department of Indian Affairs and Northern Development is regularly petitioned for new reserves so that unhappy family groups can strike off on their own and leave the conflicts behind. Similarly, when youth gangs form, they generally do so along family lines and thereby perpetuate long-standing antagonisms. Band elections show the same divisions in most communities as rival families vie for power, forming and unforming alliances as the situation dictates in an effort to keep the other groups from power.

On a broader scale, the history of Native peoples in North America is also a history of conflict, of battles over territory as one group sought to dislodge another by force from areas thought to be more advantageous. When Native people speak of their proud warrior tradition, they are invoking memories not just of standing up to the European invaders but of battles between different tribal groups. I read with fascination the portion of Samuel Hearne's diary which covers his trip up the Coppermine River in 1769-72, for it is full of descriptions of inter-tribal raids, battles, kidnappings and enslavements. Most gruesome of all was the encounter between his Indian guides and a group of "Eskimos" at the mouth of the Coppermine. Hearne's guides ambushed and killed the Eskimo men, women and children with what he perceived to be intense glee. His recounting of his helplessness to intervene in the slaughter is climaxed by his account of an Eskimo woman clinging to his boots while his guides impaled her with spears and, before delivering the killing blows at Hearne's request, ridiculed his "softness" by asking if he now desired an Eskimo wife. He gave the location a name it still carries: Bloody Falls.

I mention such incidents not to make a case for the moral superiority of one civilization over another. Our history, too, contains periods of prolonged national, racial or religious savagery, from the Crusades right through to Northern Ireland today, from the Spanish Inquisition to Hitler's ovens. I mention these events because they appear to stand in such contrast to the ethics of respect and non-interference discussed thus far, ethics which appear to have been common to all Native groups across the continent, no matter how much they warred with each other. If they shared so many beliefs barring even the verbal expression of hostility, how could they too have so regularly fought the same kinds of territorial, racial or religious wars that mark western history?

The answer, not surprisingly, lies in the dynamics of in-group/out-group behaviour which are common to all societies. The challenge for Native people is identical to the one that all people face: expanding the definition of the in-group so that rules of cooperation, tolerance and respect are extended to include everyone on this crowded planet. What makes their challenge more immediate and more daunting is that they were suddenly *required* to live side by side with their former out-groups in communities which were created, by us, almost overnight. They have simply not had the time to make the requisite adjustment.

Ironically, the strongest unifying force for Native people today is our presence. Just as our governments mask internal divisions by raising the spectre of an external threat, so too Native communities and organizations use "us", the non-Native world, as the threat which demands unity and the abandonment of internal antagonisms.

I wish to stress how difficult it has been, and continues to be, for Native communities and organizations to act with the degree

✦

of cooperation we expect of them. Each family lost, if you will, the luxury of in-group insularity and was asked, very suddenly, to set aside its historical definitions of "we" and "they". It was not a process of evolution in the North, as it was among agricultural people in upstate New York who coalesced to form the Six Nations Confederacy. There was no opportunity to discern gradually the advantages of increased cooperation and alliance and to respond with well-thought-out changes in attitude. They were simply thrown together, by the European settlers, and expected to do better than we would in similar circumstances.

What is of particular interest in their struggle to devise systems of ethics appropriate to larger groups is the possibility that they may be able to transform many of their original, and very humane, family-centred ethics into the prevailing ethics not only of entire communities but also of the Native population as a whole.

I think here of things like their tendency to emphasize rehabilitation when people go astray, to feel community shame as strongly as we feel family shame and, perhaps more importantly, to take community responsibility for the health and well-being of each individual as seriously as we take it within each family. If, as we are seeing now in the context of dealing with family violence and sexual abuse, community leaders issue a call for a concerted community response, will it fall on ears that are attuned to such overtures by conditioning from times when family health over-rode individual concerns? Will they be successful in expanding the concept of the in-group to include a continent-wide people, without getting side-tracked onto the path of "rugged individualism"?

In our society we have had the time to develop rules governing cooperative relationships between various groups, second-tier ethics, so to speak, to deal with friendly but arms-length relationships. Many Native groups, on the other hand, are attempting to transfer their intra-family ethics forward, without altering them, into their social and political lives as well. In other words, they are attempting to expand the definition of the in-group (while trusting all others to do so as well) so that traditional family ethics become the ethics controlling all their affairs.

✦

I don't for a moment suggest that this has been accomplished yet, or that there are signs of this effort in all communities. It is much more tentative than that. In fact, most communities are still characterized more by division of one sort or another. Some communities, however, have been racked by such extreme levels of violence and despair that simple survival demanded fundamental change. In some of those cases, the people involved ended up trying to define and give voice to their own ethical heritage simply as part of a plea for understanding. As soon as the fighting stopped long enough for people to listen with open hearts and minds, they were caught by surprise, for they began to recognize values and commandments which had always been their own. It was almost a matter of ethical resonance, as if in seeing others accurately they were also seeing images of themselves. This phenomenon is most apparent at conferences involving Native people from across the country. While they learn much about differences between the various tribal groups, the more powerful learning involves discovering the extent to which they share common ethical precepts. This discovery, in turn, seems to inspire a growing self-esteem right across the Native population in Canada. As each individual speaks of ethical commandments learned from his or her parents, the words strike chords of recognition in others, and the end result is a growing conviction in a common, widespread and worthy Native culture which all have a duty to reinforce at home.

The emphasis on consultation and consensus is one of those common traits which, while it was formed in the context of extended family decision-making, is being carried forward into larger arenas, including Native political organizations. When the Manitoba Legislature met to vote on the so-called Meech Lake amendments to the Canadian Constitution in 1990, for instance, and it came time for Elijah Harper to state his position as the only Native member of that house, he did not do so without elaborate consultation. Contrary to the suspicions of Jeffrey Simpson, a national columnist for the Toronto *Globe and Mail* newspaper, Mr. Harper was by no means a puppet whose strings were being pulled by political activists and cause-oriented lawyers. In fact, he had been engaged in a very laborious, time-consuming and *sincere*

✦

process of consultation, mostly by telephone, with Native people from across the country. Ironically, that careful process was documented in the same newspaper the very next day by one of its reporters, Geoffrey Stevens. He had watched it closely, and came away musing that perhaps the entire constitutional impasse might have been avoided had the Prime Minister and his cabinet shown a similar concern for consulting and forging a consensus before staking out *their* rigid positions. It is, without question, a very lengthy process when the group that is seeking consensus involves so many diverse interests; in the Native view, however, taking *no* position is preferable to taking one that has not been built by the broadest consultation possible.

I once had a long conversation with the young Chief of a reserve near Kenora about the difficulties he faced in trying to create conditions where such consensus might be possible. His community had sunk to the bottom in terms of violence and substance abuse, and only recently, with his help, had begun to pull itself up. As he spoke of the band council's plans for new housing in the community, it became clear that he was setting things up so that different families were going to congregate in separate areas. It was his hope that this would reduce the occasions for inter-family friction. I asked him if, by encouraging this return to a traditional separation along family lines, he was not slowing down the process of learning to work together. I referred to another very troubled reserve where groups had always lived separately along a length of highway, so separately that there was in reality no sense of community at all. In their case, the separation had indeed blocked any chance of developing community responses to community problems. It also led to the situation where young men from one area of the reserve would regularly travel to the other for the express purpose of accosting the women there, often passing on the highway young men from the other group going in the opposite direction for exactly the same purpose. He responded that he would not attempt the new settlement plan except that he had strong Elders from each family on council, people who could be counted upon to cooperate with each other and to work hard within their respective families to persuade everyone to forget their old suspicions and animosities. This breathing space, he

✦

hoped, would give everyone the opportunity to learn that, as he phrased it, "attacking each other is attacking ourselves." The in-group had to be expanded in each person's heart first, and this would happen only over time.

When we hear Native leaders speak so movingly about working together, about being brothers to each other, I think we fail to recognize that they are directing their exhortations to their own people as much as to us. When we see the people on reserve councils or in larger Native organizations sinking into paralysis through internal divisions, we should not be surprised. Many of our own organizations are similarly paralysed, even though they have in some cases existed for centuries. Native people are writing their own new rules for cooperation among themselves, rules that can only be refined and accepted by all over considerable time. We have a duty, I suggest, to continue to foster their various organizations, for even as they deal with particular issues they are also coming to grips with the more fundamental issue of developing mechanisms for consensus-building and cooperation among historically separate groups. It is possible that the patterns and mechanisms Native people develop will be substantially different from ours, much more closely tied to those employed within extended families for thousands of years. That is the experience they are drawing from and it is their common heritage. What emerges may be founded upon and demonstrate a kind of mutual respect that no longer seems to govern our relations with our own leaders.

There is one more context in which I hope that family-centred ethics will be used as a model to influence the workings of the larger society. Although I intend to address this context at length in the final chapter, I touch upon it here because it flows naturally from what has just been said. I refer to the fact that while our society frequently pays lip service to the ideal of "the family of man", we, as members of that society, regularly act in ways which ignore or defy that declaration. Our prisons, our failure to adequately fund therapeutic measures for persons in emotional, mental or physical need, even the cries of opposition we are accustomed to hearing whenever a halfway house or group home is proposed for a residential neighbourhood—all of these

✦

attempts to deny our responsibility suggest not dedication to the notion of a family of man but instead a readiness to discard those who disturb us. This is not the attitude that I see in Native communities today, and it is not the attitude they are attempting to foster. If nothing else, Native approaches may succeed in reminding us of how far we have strayed from notions of collective responsibility and the universal brotherhood of man.

A particularly striking example of this difference is found in a 1990 report by the Ontario Native Women's Association on the high incidence of physical and sexual abuse of women on the remote reserves. The picture that the authors of this report painted was a desperate one, for they estimated that between sixty and eighty percent of women on these reserves suffered such physical abuse at one time or another. Their recommendations, however, did not include jail as a response. Instead, they recommended the establishment of places of immediate safety and then of "healing houses" for the women, their children *and for the men who had abused them.* They were convinced that such behaviour demonstrated that the abuser, too, is in need of community aid to help him deal in constructive ways with the forces that led him, usually in a drunken state, to act as he had. The authors of the report were clearly focussing on the fact that each dysfunctional person would always remain a part of his or her community, no matter what happened to them in the short run. For the sake of both community safety and the felt duty towards others in need of assistance, they opposed any policy that would categorize such abusers as incorrigible enemies of the community and lead to their being written off.

There is, in this view, a basic correspondence between approaches taken towards disruptive people and approaches taken towards the natural order. We, on our linear path, live under the illusion that we can simply throw away the byproducts of production, distribution and consumption that distrub us. We seem to take the same attitude towards those people who disturb us. We pretend that we can put them out of sight too, that they will never come back to haunt or disturb us, and that we can ignore whatever factors produced their dysfunction. Just as Native people traditionally viewed their relationship with the environment as a circular one requiring much attention to maintaining a healthy balance, so too, I suggest, do they approach people, as "resources" which all will need, and as entities which are worthwhile in themselves and for that reason alone deserve to be nurtured. Discarding people was a last resort, taken only when all other measures had failed and their continued presence posed an unacceptable risk to the community. Although this is an attitude which would not prompt surprise when it comes to family situations, I see Native people trying to maintain and foster it as the essential attitude in multi-family communities and, indeed, across the country. They have not yet met that goal, but they are moving in that direction. They still face many hurdles, not the least of which is inter-family hostility, but if they continue to cultivate the wisdom of their Elders, this is the path that will be followed.

As a preface to the final chapter, I must mention again the workshop that a northern reserve organized to discuss the sexual abuse of children. One of the participants was a woman from another Ojibway community who came to speak of the abuse that she had suffered as a child, and of the different approaches she had taken to try to deal with it. She indicated that she wanted to speak in Ojibway, not in English, for two reasons. First, she wanted to be certain that the Elders who were present would be able to understand what she said.

The second reason, however, was more fundamental than that. As she described it, Ojibway was a "softer" language than English when it came to describing such things. Ojibway did not contain expressions for such concepts as "the accused" or "the offender", concepts which have the effect of stigmatizing the person involved. Ojibway terms, she told me, would not amount to "labels" like our words would, for they would not characterize the person but describe, in gentle terms, what he or she had done. They are verb-oriented expressions, not categorizing nouns, and as such they do not "freeze" a person within a particular classification for the rest of his life. With their emphasis on activity, these words instead emphasize process rather than state, thus helping the person who hears them to understand that all of life is a process and every person is a "thing-which-is-becoming", as opposed to a "thing-which-is". From this perspective, no one can be written off because of what they did at a particular moment in time. Instead, since each person is always "someone-in-the-making", it becomes everyone's duty to assist in that process.

As this language-based illustration suggests, it is quite likely that there is a different view of the definition of man at work here, one which serves as a foundation for every aspect of Native culture discussed thus far. I know I cannot capture or convey this definition completely. In fact, not being able to speak any Native languages severely limits my ability to gain more than a rudimentary understanding. I can only provide the clues that I have observed and do my best to point in the direction which they seem to indicate. I take considerable solace from the fact that the many Native people who reviewed the manuscript in advance of publication seemed to feel I was at least on the right path.

CHAPTER 10

THE DOCTRINE OF ORIGINAL SANCTITY

I have saved the most difficult topic for the last. This final discussion will centre not on particular rules of conduct but on a fundamental perception of the nature of humanity. If this perception prevails, then certain attitudes cannot help but be formed, and the particular rules of conduct discussed so far will inevitably follow.

It might have been more logical to explore this perception in Chapter 1. I found, however, that I was unable to describe it with the fullness it deserved until I had first explored its various manifestations. I hope that it can now be seen for what it really is: the foundation of a cohesive philosophy that provides the force and rationale for all of the cultural imperatives discussed previously. I should note as well that as this final chapter proceeds it will serve to modify, expand and even *alter* earlier statements about particular ethical commandments, for discussions which did not include knowledge of this fundamental perception of humanity could not help but be both incomplete and potentially misleading. As I indicated at the outset, the pattern of my exploration is, because of its subject matter, a circular one requiring suspension of judgement until the last word is said.

✦

In this chapter I specifically want to ask Native people to be patient with my attempt, as an outsider, to explore some very central—and sensitive—issues. I know that I will not be able to describe them with the fullness or accuracy they deserve, but I hope that I am at least moving *towards* understanding them. I also feel very strongly that I want to share what little I have learned with those who have not had the benefit of watching and listening to Elders as they go about their work.

A great deal of my learning has taken place at the Sandy Lake Reserve in northwestern Ontario. That Oji-Cree community of twelve hundred people presented a justice proposal to the Ministry of the Attorney General of Ontario in the summer of 1989. Written by Mr. Josias Fiddler, a former Chief, the proposal spoke at length about community aspirations in the justice field, about how the community looked at people who came into conflict with the law, and about their suggestions for incorporating a Native voice in the justice process. It was their wish that we begin an experiment aimed at finding ways, in their words, to "marry" the traditional Native justice system and the existing outside system. Central to that effort was the request that three Elders, to be selected by the community, join the court and participate in the sentencing of people found to have broken the law.

The proposal was accepted, and in June of 1990 the Attorney General, Ian Scott, travelled to Sandy Lake to be present at the investiture of those Elders. It was a moving ceremony, presided over by Justice of the Peace Charlie Fisher, with the Elders wearing their red, pullover ribbon shirts, symbols of the esteem in which the community held them.

During the ceremony Charlie Fisher explained that traditional Native common law was comprised of only five words. The first was "Respect", which meant respect for all things, for all people, for the Creator, and for yourself. The next two were "Good" and "Bad". If you learned respect, you would then know what was bad and what was good. The last two words were "Good Life", for if you understood the law and followed it, a good life would be the result.

I also wrote down the words of one of the Elders, Abel Rae, when he accepted the new role his community had requested of

✦

him. He promised, and urged his fellow Elders to promise, to "think of the value of the life that we are dealing with."

Those three Elders have been sitting with the court since June of 1991. As I mentioned earlier, we place long trestle tables in such a way that they form a large square. The judge, his clerk and his reporter occupy one side of the square. To his right are the Elders and an interpreter. Directly across from the judge is where the defence lawyers, offenders and their families sit, together with probation officers and others who may wish to address the court. The fourth part of the square is occupied by the Crown Attorney and those police officers involved in the cases at hand. Everything is translated so that everyone in attendance can understand what is taking place. If a conviction is entered, the next issue is the sentence thought to be most appropriate. It is at this point that the Elders have an opportunity to speak to the accused and family members, and to make recommendations about the sentence they believe will be most productive from a community perspective. The Elders bring to the court their knowledge of the accused and his or her family circumstances, and their appreciation of the specific events which might have contributed to the commission of the offense. They often meet with the accused, the victim, and their families in advance of court; the court does what it can to adjourn cases so that they have the time they consider necessary to investigate all possible alternatives.

In the year and a half that the project has been going, I have begun to see some very clear differences between the approaches of the Elders and those which characterize our southern courts. As I expected, the Elders seldom speak about the transgression itself, about the past. They focus instead upon the future, upon restoration of peaceful relations. They do not speak of punishment, but they do focus upon compensation and restitution to the victim, upon "making things right again". They also ask the accused, as a sign of respect and community support, to donate some money to support a volunteer community security force which assists the police in maintaining the community curfew, in detecting alcohol coming into the community (it being a "dry" reserve where liquor is banned), and in dealing with those who become intoxicated and present problems either to themselves or to others. They do not make threatening noises about what might happen to offenders if they repeat their misbehaviour. Instead, they remind them of how important they are to their family and their community, and about the contributions they can make in the future. They also talk about the help that they and others stand ready to provide to assist each person to realize his or her potential. At every step it seems as though the underlying message is that each person before the court can, with guidance, counselling and sustained effort on their own part, come closer to realizing the *goodness* that lies within them.

After observing the Elders' approach for several months, I started to listen more closely to the ways in which we speak to offenders in our regular courts. We repeatedly remind them of the destructive results of their behaviour, something I have never heard the Elders do. We threaten offenders with heavier sentences if they repeat their offences. We tell them it will likely be very hard for them to curb their bad habits, cure their addictions or control their violent impulses. Although we do speak of rehabilitation, we seem to do so in a tone which suggests that we doubt they will make it. We also, obviously, rely very heavily on punishment.

The more I thought about the very different approach of the Elders, the more I remembered a paragraph in the original Sandy Lake proposal to the government:

> Probably one of the most serious gaps in the system is the different perception of wrongdoing and how to treat it. In the non-Native society, committing a crime seems to mean that the individual is a bad *person* and therefore must be punished. ...The Indian communities view a wrongdoing as a misbehaviour which requires teaching, or an illness which requires healing. (emphasis added)

I began to wonder about this assertion that, to us, the commission of a crime seems to define the individual as a bad person. I began to wonder whether we see *all* people, not just those who break laws or commit other anti-social acts, in the same light. Could it be that we view people as being defined not by essential strength and goodness but by weakness and, if not outright malevolence,

✦

then at least indifference to others? Our judicial lectures and religious sermons seem to dwell on how hard we will have to work
not to give in to our *base* instincts. Is that how we see ourselves,
and each other?

Whether that is accurate or not as a general proposition, the
Elders of Sandy Lake (and elsewhere) certainly do not speak from
within that sort of perspective. At every step they tell each
offender they meet with not about how hard he'll have to work to
control his base self but instead how they are there to help him
realize the goodness that is within him.

In short, the Elders seem to do their best to convince people
that they are one step away from heaven instead of one step away
from hell. They define their role not within anything remotely like
the doctrine of original sin but within another, diametrically opposite doctrine which I will call the doctrine of original sanctity.

Sceptics can argue that what I am talking about here is a distinction without substance, an argument with no more significance
than the philosophers' debate about whether a glass of water is
half-full or half-empty. I do not think that is the case. I think the
difference between the two emphases is critical.

The freely chosen responses to criminal activity illustrate
the differences which flow from adopting each of the two perspectives. If it is your conviction that people live one short step
from hell, that it is more natural to sin than to do good, then
your response as a judicial official will be to use terror to prevent the taking of that last step backward. You will be quick to
threaten offenders with dire consequences should they "slide
back" into their destructive ways. In fact, a band councillor
once asked me directly why our courts came into his community when all we wanted to do was, in his words, "terrorize my
people with jail and fines". If, by contrast, it is your conviction
that people live one step away from heaven, you will be more
likely to respond by coaxing them gently forward, by encouraging them to progress, to realize the goodness within them. The
use of coercion, threats or punishment by those who would
serve as guides to goodness would seem a denial of the very
vision that inspires them. And that, I suggest, is how the Elders
see it.

✦

The more fundamental aspect of this different perspective has to do with the proper focus for law and for the courts. A belief system centred on the innate sinfulness of man, having conceded a base nature, will then concentrate its efforts on proscribing harmful *acts*. It will, in essence, tell people "We know what you are, and we can't change that, but we can and will demand that you not *do* X, Y or Z, or else we will step in." The law, as a result, will focus on one's actions and essentially ignore one's state of mind. The countervailing belief system, focused upon the innate goodness of man, will focus upon *pre*scribing states of *mind*, states to be attained in a progression towards ultimate self-realization. It will focus not upon the prohibiting of acts but on the attainment of spiritual states. Good acts, it is assumed, will inevitably follow.

This, I have learned, is what Charlie Fisher was telling us when he spoke of the five words that made up traditional common law. One aspired to maintaining the spiritual state of respect, following which one's activities will of necessity be constructive rather than destructive.

A young Native man at an aboriginal policing conference in Edmonton, Alberta, in 1990, asked me, "Why does your law, from the Ten Commandments to the Criminal Code, speak only of what people should not *do*? Why don't your laws speak to people about what they should *be*?" When I heard that question, my first reaction was that he was obviously unaware of the distance we maintain between church and state, between religious matters and those of the secular justice system. We place all of our concern about what people should be in the religious category, while concerns about what people actually do are thought to be properly the subject of the judicial system. I now believe, however, that he had *not* confused these two categories. Instead, he was insisting that a justice system ought to perform both roles. To the extent that it focused only upon activity, he was suggesting that it must be declared a failure. Another Elder at that same conference declared, more in sorrow than in anger, "We know you have a *legal* system; we're just not sure it's a *justice* system."

I recall one sentencing at Sandy Lake that illustrated the difference between the two approaches. When a young man was

✦

found sitting on a tree stump after midnight, highly intoxicated, he was charged under the band bylaw with being intoxicated on the reserve. After he entered a guilty plea, the issue became what the court should do with him. In our regular courts, such an offence would attract an automatic light fine, and that would be the end of it. In the eyes of the Sandy Lake Elders, however, sentencing was far from automatic. Their focus was not upon his act but upon how he came to be in that state. They had made their enquiries and determined that the young man's wife had left the community with their infant child to take up residence on another reserve. There were a number of difficulties in the marriage that, in the Elders' view, had never been addressed. The recommended sentence, therefore, involved not only counselling for the young man's alcohol abuse, but counselling for his marriage problems as well. The Elders indicated that they would do what they could to persuade his wife to return so that the family as a whole could attempt, with the assistance of counselling, to overcome its difficulties. Such a sentence was, in our terms, relatively severe, for the rehabilitative measures amounted to a severe intrusion into the young man's life. Our judicial response would have been to assess a fine and send him on his way; such a response would clearly justify the words of the councillor I reported earlier when he declared that our courts "just take our money out in fines or our people out to jail, and leave us with the problem".

The Sandy Lake Elders, by contrast, feel it is both their duty and their right to probe behind particular acts and to put in place measures they think might get at the root of the problem. That root, it bears repeating, is the lack of harmony within the individual that prompts the harmful act in the first place.

It is worth noting that the Elders respond in much the same fashion when the act is much more serious in nature. When the offence involves an assault, they try to go behind it to investigate the context in which the parties live, the frustrations they face, the resources they have to deal with them, and the need for outside assistance. A knife assault and wounding frequently result in the same kinds of sentencing recommendations that accompany simple intoxication charges. Those recommendations, without fail, focus almost exclusively upon rehabilitation for the accused

✦

and for those other people closest to him. Retribution or punishment does not seem to cross their minds.

The other significant aspect of the Elders' approach is its possible impact on each offender's self-esteem. Virtually every court-ordered psychiatric assessment I have seen, whether it deals with a Native or non-Native offender, concludes that a major contributing cause to the unlawful act was low self-esteem. A multitude of studies point to self-esteem problems as an important source of violence, especially against women and children. The denigration and abuse of others—the demonstration of power over them—is in large part a desperate assertion of self. Most sexual crimes show the same root: the real issue is not sex but power, not uncontrolled sensuality but the use of force by those so empty of self-esteem that they will do anything to convince others (and themselves) that they are in fact a force to be reckoned with. It is almost as if each assaultive act is done to be able to state, "See me! See what I can *do*, and you will see that I *am*!" That is not the entire explanation, of course, but it constitutes a significant part of it. Self-esteem, then, a psychological or mental issue, is indeed an important component of the background material that helps the judge determine an appropriate sentence, no matter where the court is sitting.

If that is so, then perhaps we should be asking what impact the court process has on that self-esteem. The Elders seem to think it counter-productive to tell an offender constantly how much damage he has done, how he has hurt others, how it is his failure to control his harmful impulses that is to blame. Instead, they seem to make a deliberate attempt to improve each offender's self-esteem by reminding him of his potential for goodness, of his capacity to move forward, with help, towards self-fulfilment. Their constant emphasis is upon respect, *including respect for one's self*. By offering their assistance and counselling, they demonstrate their belief in each person and their faith that they can get themselves back on the path to a good life.

From this perspective, we see once again how ethics barring criticism or reference to past mistakes makes logical sense. To the extent that any discussion focuses upon failure or upon harm already done—or even upon simple inadequacy—it will only

✦

detract from the effort to create, in each person's heart, the belief that he is "good" and, more importantly, always capable of "better". The soft words used to describe even traumatic events do not label or stigmatize a person; they too speak in terms of the process of self-attainment. The quicker a particular mistake is compensated for and forgiven, and the balance thus restored, the quicker each offender can resume his natural progress. From the Native perspective, even the notion of a criminal record is seen as counter-productive, for it serves only to remind of failure.

We can also see why the Elders favour the use of instructive parables over direct criticism. Criticism focuses almost entirely upon the past, and upon failures in that past, while enlightening parables instead serve to coax people forward towards better ways of doing things in the future.

This same emphasis and approach is apparent when Native people question our extensive reliance upon jails in the criminal justice system. The Sandy Lake justice proposal to the Ontario government expressed their view that the act of committing a crime meant that the offender was already estranged from his community, at least in a social sense. It was their fear that this estrangement would only be intensified if offenders were then removed physically from the community and placed in distant jails. Time spent in jail, in their eyes, would only result in the creation of a *more* socially alienated, defiant and isolated individual, one who would be even more difficult to restore into the community. In their words, the challenge they faced was "most importantly to *stop* the process of isolating people from their community".

The Sandy Lake proposal also made it clear that outsiders have not yet understood what Native people really mean when they call our justice system adversarial. They are not referring to our use of two lawyers arguing as professional adversaries before an impartial judge in search of truth and fair treatment. Instead, they are referring to the fact that our system responds to misbehaviour by imposing punishment on offenders, treating *them* as adversaries of society at large. As the proposal phrased it: "The system itself is adversarial in nature. It stresses the removal of a problem (that is, a person) rather than the solving of a problem within a community context." That "problem" is defined by the

✦

Elders not in terms of past acts but of the continuing mental state of the accused, with particular focus upon the degree to which he has lost respect for himself and for others. The proposal stated: "There must be respect for the Creator and for all of creation, including the environment, other people, other people's property and oneself." The function of a justice system, in their view, must be to assist a return to that mental state. The frequent use of phrases referring to restoration, to making a person whole again, to re-establishing harmony, all suggest a vision in which people are seen, as in traditional times, as born to goodness and harmony rather than to sin.

I don't believe that this emphasis on re-building self-esteem by positive reinforcement is merely a tactic, a response chosen consciously to promote social peace. I believe instead that it is a necessary manifestation of a core conviction: the conviction that each person is derived from the Creator, is defined by the Creator's goodness, and can aspire to a spiritual sanctity that approximates, at least in kind, that possessed by the Creator. When a person misbehaves and causes harm, it does not prove that he is a malevolent creature, only that he is in need of assistance to bring himself back to himself again. Furthermore, within this belief system, each person and each community is under the Creator's duty to offer that assistance when it is needed.

I want to return for a moment to some of the ethics of traditional times that I discussed in Chapter 3. I examined, among others, the ethic forbidding the expression of criticism or anger. There was, of course, a practical reason for that prohibition: the need to maintain the highest possible level of cooperation in the struggle for survival. There was also the consideration of interaction with the spirit world and the belief that one's own thoughts might not be private. It was for that reason important not to think things which might lead to hostility or taking offence. I suggest that such practical concerns were not the only source of such ethics. The larger contributor was, in all likelihood, the belief system which centred upon the conviction that man was innately good and could, with effort and dedication, refine his goodness to approximate that of the beneficent Creator. The true prohibition

✦

was not simply against the *expression* of criticism or anger but against letting such feelings grow within you in the first place.

For one thing, such feelings were inappropriate, in that the failings of others were just that, mere shortcomings that could, with guidance and effort, be overcome. They were understood and tolerated as inevitable events in each person's path to fulfilment. They were occasions for help and understanding, not censure or blame. Just as importantly, the feeling of anger or the desire to criticize were signs of one's own spiritual imperfection, a signal that a person was still permitting disruptive and unworthy thoughts to control his own spirit. Permitting such feelings to take hold could only be seen as a sign of the need to work harder towards the patience, understanding and generosity that signified the attainment of spiritual health. Such negative thoughts and feelings were akin to spiritual poisons which would contaminate each person's essential goodness.

In that sense, these ethics were more fundamental than they first appeared, for they went beyond a concern with the harmful practical consequences of permitting angry or critical thoughts to be expressed. Instead, they focused on each person's spiritual health, upon his or her spiritual self-realization.

At the beginning of the book, I asked for my readers' patience. I suggested that various things might be inaccurately or incompletely described in the first chapters, but that they would come to be seen more fully as the exploration progressed. We are in just such a situation here. I have always spoken of traditional ethics as rules which *prohibited* the saying, doing or feeling of particular things. I suggest now that those ethics did not take the form of prohibitions as we understand the term. Instead, I suggest that they took the form of exhortations to the attainment of an *un*-poisoned spirit, that they were understood not as rules *against* one thing or another, but as insistent exhortations *towards* something, namely, self-realization. Dwelling on past misfortune was not only counterproductive, resulting in diminished attention, energy and will. It was also spiritually counter-productive in that it weighed the spirit down and retarded its growth.

This preference for forgetting was, in all likelihood, not expressed as a prohibition against self-indulgence but as a gentle

✦

coaxing towards a freeing of the spirit so that it might continue its journey towards a purity that participates, as it was meant to, in the purity of the Creator. Recall here the words of the young man at the justice conference who asked why all our laws spoke of what people should not *do* and were silent about what people should *be*.

As I suggested earlier, a philosophy centred upon the innate goodness of man cannot help but lead to particular kinds of responses to anti-social acts. People will view the offender as having had his basic nature temporarily poisoned or perverted by some outside influence, his natural harmony and balance disrupted. The result of his act will matter less than what the act says about the extent to which that interior balance has been displaced. The appropriate response of a true justice system will then be one that focuses upon the restoration of that internal balance, not the imposition of punishment which can only make things worse. The offender's external circumstances will be examined to see if the stresses which surround him can be lessened. At the same time, his internal condition will also be assessed to so that healing measures can be provided to restore his spiritual balance. Spiritual contaminants such as anger, jealousy and fear must be removed so that people can return to their natural state of harmony and respect.

This second effort, cleansing the spirit, was central, for until that was accomplished the individual could not progress on his spiritual journey. As I acknowledged earlier, I have very little knowledge of traditional cleansing or healing practices. My only experience in this connection involves participation in a sweat-lodge ceremony at the Sandy Lake Reserve. I must say, however, that I found it both a humbling and an empowering experience. I could feel its potential for spiritual cleansing. With the permission of the keeper of the sweat, Mr. Josias Fiddler (the same man who authored the Sandy Lake justice proposal), I would like to try to explain what I mean.

About a dozen people in bathing suits (in former times they sat naked) gathered inside a small dome made of canvas supported by willow branches dug into the clay. Judge Don Fraser and I were the only two outsiders. In the middle of the enclosure was a circular pit into which fire-heated rocks were placed by "helpers" who otherwise remained outside. In this sweat, there were four "rounds", in between which the canvas flaps were raised to let out the steam, we all relaxed with drinks of cold water, and we were told of the theme for the following round. Then new rocks were brought in from a large fire-pit outside, more herbs were sprinkled upon them, the flaps were closed by the helpers, and the next round began. The sweat had begun, of course, with a pipe ceremony once we were assembled inside.

Each of the rounds was dedicated to a particular theme, including respect for the Elders and their value to all, respect for the planet and its richness, respect for the promise of children and their need for our patience and guidance, and respect for each individual's internal harmony and the need to pay close attention to maintaining its purity. As each round began, the canvas flaps were closed, leaving us in complete darkness as soon as the glow of the new rocks diminished. The Chanter then began a series of established prayers dedicated to the particular theme. It was explained to us that all participants were to pray, out loud, either by joining the Chanter or by using our own language to express our own thoughts. We were also instructed that we had to concentrate all our thoughts on such prayers; if we felt we could not take the heat as it grew, it meant only that we were not concentrating adequately on the theme at hand.

I do not know *how* various things happened in the darkness of that little space. In fact, I tried to close off my western mind and ignore that kind of question, for it is entirely irrelevant. Instead, I want to try to explain *what* happened, and how it made me feel, from both a physiological and a psychological perspective. Most striking was the fact that each successive physiological state had an impact upon my psychological state, and the two seemed to join together into what I can only describe as a spiritual force.

From a strictly sensory point of view, there was intense stimulation. The temperature rose swiftly as water turned to steam on the hot rocks; sweat began to run down every part of my skin. A variety of smells invaded my nostrils as herbs were burned. The chanting of a dozen voices set up a rhythmic, pulsing energy in that small space, punctuated now and then by loud rattles and

✦

shrill whistles that came at unpredictable intervals and from varying locations. Now and then sprinkles of cold water fell upon my exposed skin. On occasion, the cold water came in small waves that broke upon my head and back as I knelt before the pit. At other times what felt like a scalding wind enveloped me as steam-laden air moved around the circular walls and penetrated the thin layer of body-cooled air which built against my skin. The variety, pace and impact of the various stimuli kept my senses constantly on the alert.

What made the experience unique, however, was the darkness in which I knelt. Because I could see absolutely nothing, there was no way to anticipate what kind of stimulus was coming, or when. There was no choice but to simply *accept* whatever sensation came next through the darkness, whether it was a chant, a sprinkle, a whistle, a wave, a rattle or a scorching wind.

It was the psychological aspect of coping with such unforeseeable sensory stimuli which made the most impact on me. At first, not being able to anticipate the next sensation was, if not frightening, then at least very disconcerting. Before long, however, that changed. There was no choice but to accept. Once this attitude of acceptance took over, the various stimuli were no longer guarded against; the psychological posture was instead one of taking each stimulus as it came and enjoying the way it washed over me, in the sense of welcoming its capacity to have an impact upon me. It became, in a sense, for each participant, a celebration of one's sensual capacities. It was a powerful combination of being humbled (in the sense that you had no power over what was coming next, not even to anticipate and steel yourself against it), and of being empowered (by discovering that, with mental concentration upon the prayer at hand, you could not only survive very intense physical stimulation but also become in some fashion energized by the stimulation of it all). It was, in a strange way, victory over your own anxieties and fears achieved through adopting a stance of utter passivity, which victory was then accompanied by sensory delight. Such victory, it cannot be forgotten, was achieved through mental concentration, and concentration upon themes of personal re-dedication to the worth of all things. It was a combination of intense sensory and spiritual celebration undertaken in

✦

a posture of humbled acceptance, and it was a very powerful combination indeed.

It is important to remember that I shared this experience with about a dozen other people crowded together inside that canvas dome. During each round the darkness made them invisible to me, but their presence remained strong as their prayers joined the mix of chants, whistles and rattles in the steamy air. All of us, consciously or unconsciously, joined in the rhythm of the chant, following its tempo and its changing volume. There was a joining together of other spirits in common survival (it did get hot!) and common re-dedication, an intertwining in voice, experience, thought and determination. It was hard not to feel a spiritual closeness. When, at the very end, the flaps were thrown back, cool night air soothed us all and plates of orange slices and cookies were passed around the circle; even outsiders like the judge and I felt distictly joined to all the others.

I need hardly mention how much more powerful such a ceremony would be to people who fully understood the symbolism of the four colours of ribbons from the willow branches representing the four founding races, the pointing of the pipe to honour the four winds, and the thoughts, pleas and promises being expressed in each of the chants. If the experience struck me, in my ignorance of so many such things, with as much force as it did, their experience must have been significantly more profound. It is interesting, though, that the profundity of the occasion did not seem to require the dour denial of individuality which so often characterizes the ceremonies of my own culture, for between rounds there was lots of gentle kidding going on, together with good-natured complaints about joints getting stiff from kneeling, the failure of the steam to have much of an impact on well-fed bellies, and the like.

This psychological posture of what felt like *vibrant passivity* was very new to me. In fact, the phrase itself seems almost a contradiction in terms. It is, however, the only phrase which comes close to capturing my sense of the experience.

How did I feel afterwards? To use an old phrase from the sixties, I certainly felt "mellowed-out". It was much more than that, however, much more than simply feeling relaxed or emptied of

✦

consternation. It included a sense of having been cleansed of unsettling or disturbing feelings like anger, fear or anxiety. At the same time, there was a sense of those feelings being replaced by positive ones, feelings of strength and peace and celebration. At one point, as we paused between rounds for sips of cold water, we were asked what thoughts were coming to us. My response was that I had remembered the words of their Elder Abel Rae when, at his investiture, he had reminded everyone to think of the life of each person who would come before the court. I also reported a conviction that had come to me during the round, a conviction that if I felt anger inside me towards another person, it meant only that I had not grown as much as I ought to. Judge Fraser said, with the simplest eloquence, that he thought it would be wise if he could participate in such a sweat ceremony the night before each court in Sandy Lake. I don't believe either of us were trying to impress anyone; these were simply things that had come to us amidst the swirling sensory stimuli and the focus of our own thoughts on the themes presented.

In traditional times such ceremonies were a part of everyday life. Whether each person believed that he was being cleansed of evil spirits or whether he thought that he was merely discharging all his unhealthy feelings, the fact remains that he or she regularly took part in a community-sanctioned and community-run process of cleansing and re-dedication, side by side with many other members of that community. The unavoidable stresses of everyday life were routinely addressed and, if my small experience is any clue, discharged. Further, there was no shame in participating in such ceremonial cleansing, no stigma attached to seeking help in such purification. To the contrary, it was commonly agreed that everyone required such assistance, and that only a fool would reject it.

By way of contrast, I have to wonder about how contradictory many of our own approaches to mental health seem to be. On the one hand, we think of people as fighting a constant battle not to give in to base drives and instincts. On the other, we tend to stigmatize those who seek professional help. In dealing with people who have been less than successful in resisting their weaknesses, we often think of punishment as a first response. Native people,

✦

on the other hand, traditionally saw each person as essentially good, provided regular healing assistance and, when problems nevertheless remained, thought first in terms of further help. While we seem to focus on the event, on the past, and upon retribution as something that will restore the social balance, they focus steadfastly on the future, upon restoring both internal harmony and the external supports necessary to maintain that harmony. We react to crime by ostracizing the offender in jail, while they see social and spiritual estrangement as the cause of the crime. At virtually every step in the two justice processes, we "see" events differently and then, understandably, choose to respond to them differently.

The saddest part of all this is that after our arrival on this continent we did everything in our power to prevent Native people from maintaining and utilizing their own social and spiritual resources, everything we could to stop them from responding to problems in the ways they thought were most appropriate. We outlawed and denigrated their healing techniques, requiring instead that they utilize ours and, in the process, break more of their ancient commandments. More to the point, we did so just at the time when the clash between our two cultures guaranteed that these problems would be at their worst. Instead, we provided a legal system which is reactive, not proactive, which requires people to take adversarial stances against each other, and which then resorts to a punitive stance which seems wholly counterproductive in their eyes. There was no discussion in the sweat ceremony of people or events which might have caused pain, fear or anxiety; there clearly was, however, a discharge of those kinds of emotions. Just as importantly, there was at the same time a formal and communal re-dedication to the harmony, balance and respect which might avoid them in the future.

I have no doubt at all that Native people would have survived the cultural clashes which faced them upon our arrival in a significantly stronger state had they been allowed to retain their own ways of dealing with the emotional turmoil such clashes caused. The fact that they have survived as a people at all in the absence of any such techniques is, in my view, a testament to their strength as a people. With traditional techniques being brought

✦

back, often married to the better aspects of our discursive therapy, that strength can only grow exponentially.

There is one final aspect of the manner in which the Sandy Lake Elders conduct themselves in court that reveals something significant in their belief system. As I have said, they are clearly trying to bolster each offender's self-esteem in the hope that new confidence and attitudes will lead to new habits. I sense, however, that the *way* in which they attempt this is an important signal of the difference between our two cultures and their respective belief systems.

The things that the Elders point to as real accomplishments seem to centre on one particular sphere of human activity. I don't hear much about how people did in school or athletics or even trapping or hunting. Instead, I am told about what each person did to help his parents, to guide his children, to honour his Elders and to respect his traditions. There seems to be a different hierarchy of social values at work. The Elders speak of another's activity not just to show gratitude for the results of those acts but to point out what those acts suggest about his state of mind. Anyone who dedicates himself to helping others, instead of simply advancing his own interests, demonstrates a commitment to the spritual ideal of harmony and inter-connectedness.

That last word—inter-connectedness—is the key word. The philosophy states that we are not alone, nor can we go it alone. We are here not to assert dominion or to rise above the rest, but to make a contribution *with* the rest. Yes, we take what we need, but only what we need. At the same time, we try to ensure that the people and things around us continue to receive what they need as well. Success is measured not by the degree to which we subdue, but by the degree to which we serve as a conduit of sustenance for all components of creation. The successful man is the one who understands his role in that chain of sustenance and who dedicates his efforts towards maintaining harmony and balance within all creation. The degree to which his acts demonstrate that sort of understanding is the paramount consideration in assessing his success as a developing, always-progressing, human being.

The reader may argue that I have read too much into what the Elders have to say about one word, respect. Their emphasis, how-

✦

ever, on respect for oneself, respect for other people and indeed for all aspects of creation, suggests otherwise. This is especially true when this concern with respect is coupled with a deliberate lack of attention to what we would call personal accomplishments or honours. A man's or woman's success, the Elders seem to say, is to be measured solely in terms of his or her attainment of an attitude of respect. It is only within that context that a person's acts are to be viewed, and in being viewed they are not, in our sense, to be judged. If a person, by his acts, demonstrates that he has not fully attained that attitude of respect, then further guidance and support is the necessary response. If, on the other hand, a person's acts demonstrate a substantial development of that attitude, then the response is not one of praise but of celebration. He or she will be honoured, to be sure, but not because they are better than others. Instead, they will be honoured for achieving their greatest potential and, in that way, for having honoured the Creator's gift of life.

Not all Native people either understand or have chosen to live within this perspective. As the prosecutor of criminal offences in many of their communities, I know as well as anyone the degree to which that perspective no longer predominates, especially among the young. In my work with Elders, however, I can see that it is their perspective, the one they wish to restore to their people. Whether they will be able to do so in the face of substantial social disorder, and in the face of the invasion of our individualistic and materialistic culture, remains to be seen.

What we must understand is that this struggle to retrieve and restore the traditional value of respect for all creation is central to the Elders' concerns about the loss of Native culture. While they tend to cringe when their own political leaders use the term "cultural genocide", with its implications of intentional destruction, it is clear that they understand, better than anyone alive, how much has been lost over the last one hundred years. All the outlawed and denigrated facets of traditional culture—the spirit dances, the sweat-lodge and pipe ceremonies, the regular ritual offering of tobacco as a symbol of gratitude—must be seen for what they really were: tools to maintain and deepen a belief in the inter-connectedness of all things. Now that such practices are

✦

being slowly brought back, they serve a second function too, for they offer an alternative focus to that of our individualistic and materialistic value system. Native leaders and Elders are working to restore to their people, especially to their youth, the best parts of their traditional value system, the philosophy that sustained them on this continent for many thousands of years against formidable odds.

And as my own experience illustrates, they also stand ready to share their wisdom with us. For that, I suspect, we may be increasingly grateful as time goes by.

I want to close this chapter in a way that I have seen many Native people close meetings or conversations. If the atmosphere or subject matter has been sombre, someone always brings the group around with a teasing joke or a gentle and humorous story. In that vein, I offer a story I was told about a Chief from a small prairie band. It seems that the Anglican and Roman Catholic missionaries, each with their own churches in the community, had been waging a fierce battle to see which church could convert the largest number of pagan souls. The Chief found this struggle disruptive of harmony within the village, and decided that he must do something to settle the issue. His response was to write identical notes to each of the two competing churches. In those notes he promised that he would eagerly lead all of his people into *either* church, as soon as the missionaries agreed among themselves whose God was the *real* God; in the meantime, he urged them to confine the argument to themselves. I suspect that he understood them far better than they thought he did.

CONCLUSION

There is, of course, no conclusion that I can offer to the exploration undertaken in the preceding pages. It is not only impossible to define any particular culture comprehensively with either clarity or accuracy; it is also inconceivable that any culture should ever complete itself. Adaptation, evolution and, on occasion, revolution will continue to modify it. This is probably nowhere more true than in the case of the aboriginal cultures that are currently colliding with post-industrial, western societies across this continent.

To return to an earlier observation, while adaptation is essential to the growth of any culture, wholesale adoption of a foreign culture's perspectives is not. The challenge for Native people lies in choosing what they wish to adopt, what they must adapt to, and what they must either retain or restore to its original purity. In every community I visit, I see that struggle to decide which choices are most appropriate. They are, very consciously, redesigning themselves as communities by every decision they make. Each community is, in fact, experimenting with itself in a very deliberate way. They are choosing, on occasion, paths and visions that differ significantly from community to community.

Native communities are also increasingly involved in sharing their experiments with each other through Native broadcasting

✦

and print systems and through conferences across the country. One of our greatest contributions to their struggle may lie in fostering and supporting such communication, for the different Native communities need the benefit of each other's wisdom and assistance to arrive at successful new balances of adoption, adaptation, retention and restoration. As I hope I have illustrated, we can never know how great their challenges actually are in this process of search and experimentation. For that reason alone we should never presume to make for them the decisions which must be made.

I think instead that our contributions must be of a different sort. We must first understand how little we actually understand. Only then will we realize that it is impossible for us to offer anything like sound advice about what will be most productive for them. We must also acknowledge the complexity of their choices, and learn to be patient. We must expect some experiments to work and others not to work. Either way, we must agree that only they can run their own experiments, and we must work to be certain that they have the freedom to do so. We must, in this process, share our sustaining resources with them, just as they have shared the resources of this continent which now sustain us. They will, in their own fashion, ultimately find ways to become once again self-sustaining in every sense, for that is their history and their goal. That they are not there yet there should surprise no one.

Finally, we should dedicate significant resources to achieving better levels of communication in three areas. First, we need to do a better job of communicating our culture to them through mainstream educational opportunities. Only then will they be able to make informed choices about what they wish to adopt, to adapt to, or to reject. Second, we need to give them increased opportunities to communicate regularly with each other so that they can benefit from their own experiences, both from their hard-won successes and from the lessons of their failures. It is nothing short of grotesque to see the extent to which they must presently carry on their struggles in isolation from each other. Third, we need to support their communication with us, regardless of whether it is through lobby groups, joint enterprises, the arts, or even the

✦

courts. Only then can we learn of the choices they have made and so tailor any assistance measures to their definition of need, not ours.

At the same time, there may be a selfish reason for us to listen to Native leaders: we may slowly learn of approaches or values or strategies which *we* will choose to adopt or adapt for ourselves. As I have suggested, there is much of value in their notions of the proper way to relate to each other, to the universe and to oneself. How those notions might require translation to become effectively integrated into our urban, technological and bureaucratic world may well be our challenge to straighten out. Although I don't believe the predictions of imminent Armageddon that some critics propose for western culture, neither have I deluded myself into thinking that we have nothing left to learn from the wise men and women of other cultures. If I have done nothing else in this book, I hope to have established beyond controversy that there was and still is a strong, complex, sophisticated and enduring Native culture which deserves our recognition and our study.

Finally, one last comment. In my efforts to learn and translate what has been presented to me by Native people over the last several years, I have had the honour of their patience. I have also been granted the privilege of sharing in their wisdom, their faith, and their unparalleled capacity for humour. The very fact that these last two elements—faith and humour—have survived the last century is proof beyond doubt that these people maintain an approach to existence that we might be wise to investigate.

My thanks to the many Native people who have stopped to talk as I crossed their paths. I have been personally enriched by my exposure to you. I hope that the preceding pages will be received by you as a gesture of my appreciation, for that is how they are intended.

Megwetch.

SUBJECT INDEX

✦

✦

ANECDOTAL INDEX

◆

◆